COMPLETE AIR FRYER RECIPES COOKBOOK

Delicious and Healthy Meals Made Easy.

Wilma A. Bowen

Copyright © 2024 by Wilma A. Bowen

All rights reserved. No part of this publication may be reproduced, distributed, or transmitted in any form or by any means, including photocopying, recording, or other electronic or mechanical methods, without the prior written permission of the publisher, except in the case of brief quotations embodied in critical reviews and certain other noncommercial uses permitted by copyright law.

TABLE OF COMTENTS

- INTRODUCTION 8
  - BENEFITS OF AIR FRYING 9
  - TIPS FOR USING AN AIR FRYER 10
  - BREAKFAST DELIGHTS 12
    - Air Fryer Breakfast Burritos 12
    - Crispy Hash Brown Patties 13
    - Air Fried French Toast Sticks 14
    - Breakfast Sausage Links or Patties 15
    - Air Fryer Breakfast Potatoes with Peppers and Onions 16
    - Air Fryer Cinnamon Sugar Donut Holes 17
    - Blueberry Muffins with Streusel Topping 18
    - Bacon and Egg Breakfast Pockets 19
    - Banana Pancake Bites 20
    - Veggie Breakfast Quesadillas 21
    - Breakfast Egg Rolls with Sausage and Cheese 22
    - Apple Cinnamon Roll-Ups 23
    - Greek Yogurt Parfait with Granola and Berries 24
    - Spinach and Feta Mini Quiches 25
    - Air Fried Breakfast Pizza with Eggs and Bacon 26
    - Stuffed Breakfast Peppers with Eggs and Cheese 27
    - Air Fryer Breakfast Bombs filled with Ham, Egg, and Cheese 28
    - Strawberry Banana Breakfast Wraps with Nutella 29
    - Cranberry Orange Scones with Glaze 30
    - Breakfast Tater Tots Casserole with Eggs, Cheese, and Bacon 31
  - LUNCH RECIPES 32
    - Crispy Chicken Sandwiches 32
    - Air Fryer Veggie Quesadillas 33
    - Buffalo Cauliflower Wraps 34
    - Turkey Club Wraps: 35
    - Crispy Tofu Buddha Bowls 36
    - BBQ Chicken Flatbreads: 37

- Air Fryer Falafel Bowls 38
- Stuffed Portobello Mushrooms 39
- Crispy Fish Tacos 40
- Caprese Stuffed Chicken 41
- Air Fryer Sweet Potato Hash 42
- Mediterranean Veggie Wraps 43
- Crispy Coconut Shrimp 44
- Air Fryer BLT Salad 45
- Southwest Chicken Stuffed Peppers: 46

DINNER RECIPES 47

- Crispy Air Fryer Chicken Parmesan 47
- Garlic Herb Air Fryer Salmon 48
- Stuffed Bell Peppers with Quinoa and Black Beans 49
- Air Fryer Lemon Garlic Shrimp Skewers 50
- BBQ Pulled Pork Sliders with Coleslaw 51
- Crispy Air Fryer Tofu Stir-Fry 52
- Buffalo Chicken Stuffed Sweet Potatoes 53
- Crispy Breaded Air Fryer Pork Chops 54
- Vegetarian Eggplant Parmesan 55
- Honey Garlic Air Fryer Chicken Thighs 56
- Cajun Shrimp and Sausage Foil Packets 57
- Beef and Vegetable Kabobs with Chimichurri Sauce 58
- Southwest Stuffed Peppers with Ground Turkey 59
- Crispy Coconut Shrimp with Mango Salsa 60
- Teriyaki Salmon with Stir-Fried Vegetables 61

FAST FOOD FOR GOOD HEALTH 62

- Air-Fried Sweet Potato Fries 62
- Air-Fried Chicken Tenders 63
- Air-Fried Buffalo Cauliflower Wings 64
- Air-Fried Turkey Burgers: 65
- Air-Fried Coconut Shrimp 66
- Air-Fried Avocado Fries 67
- Air-Fried Turkey Burgers 68

Air-Fried Brussels Sprouts with Bacon: 69

Air-Fried Apple Crumble 70

CHICKEN AND POULTRY RECIPES 71

Crispy Air Fryer Chicken Wings 71

Honey Garlic Air Fried Chicken Drumsticks 72

Lemon Herb Air Fryer Chicken Breast 73

BBQ Ranch Air Fryer Chicken Thighs 74

Parmesan Crusted Air Fried Chicken Tenders 75

Cajun Spiced Air Fryer Turkey Breast 76

Teriyaki Glazed Air Fried Chicken Skewers 77

Buffalo Cauliflower and Chicken Bites 78

Italian Herb Marinated Air Fryer Cornish Hens 79

Garlic Butter Air Fried Turkey Meatballs 80

BEEF AND PORK 81

Air Fryer Beef Steak with Garlic Butter 81

Crispy Pork Belly Bites with Honey Glaze 82

Air Fried Beef Kebabs with Mediterranean Marinade 83

BBQ Pulled Pork Sliders with Tangy Coleslaw 84

Air Fryer Beef Fajitas with Homemade Guacamole 85

Teriyaki Glazed Pork Tenderloin Medallions 86

Beef and Pork Meatballs with Marinara Sauce 87

Air Fried Korean BBQ Beef Ribs 88

Honey Mustard Glazed Pork Chops 89

Beef and Pork Stir-Fry with Fresh Vegetables 90

APPETIZERS AND SNACKS 91

Crispy Chicken Wings: 91

Air-Fried Mozzarella Sticks 92

Sweet Potato Fries 93

Buffalo Cauliflower Bites 94

Air-Fried Onion Rings 95

Air-Fried Jalapeño Poppers (Healthy-ish Version) 96

Air-Fried Coconut Shrimp 97

Loaded Potato Skins 98

Parmesan Zucchini Fries ... 99

Avocado Egg Rolls: ... 100

FISH AND SEAFOOD RECIPES ... 101

Crispy Air Fryer Fish Fillets ... 101

Garlic Herb Shrimp Skewers: ... 102

Coconut-Crusted Air Fryer Shrimp ... 103

Lemon Garlic Air Fryer Salmon ... 104

Cajun Blackened Catfish ... 105

Sesame Ginger Glazed Mahi Mahi ... 106

Lemon Pepper Scallops ... 107

Crispy Coconut-Crusted Cod ... 108

Mediterranean Grilled Octopus: ... 109

Spicy Sriracha Glazed Shrimp ... 110

VEGETARIAN AND VEGAN DISHES ... 111

Crispy Air Fryer Falafel ... 111

Stuffed Bell Peppers ... 112

Vegetable Spring Rolls: ... 113

Vegetarian Portobello Mushroom Burgers: ... 114

Vegan Portobello Mushroom Burgers: ... 115

Crispy Tofu Nuggets (Air Fryer) ... 116

Eggplant Parmesan ... 117

Sweet Potato Tots ... 118

Coconut-Crusted Tofu (Air Fryer Recipe) ... 119

Mediterranean Stuffed Zucchini: ... 121

Quinoa and Mushroom Stuffed Zucchini ... 122

SIDES AND ACCOMPANIMENTS ... 123

Crispy Garlic Parmesan Potato Wedges ... 123

Air Fried Asparagus with Lemon Zest ... 124

Crispy Air Fryer Zucchini Fries with Marinara Sauce ... 125

Honey Glazed Carrots with Thyme ... 126

Cauliflower Buffalo Bites with Ranch Dressing ... 127

Cornbread Stuffed Jalapeños (Air Fryer Version) ... 128

Rosemary Garlic Roasted Potatoes ... 129

- Air Fryer Brussels Sprouts with Balsamic Glaze 130
- Sweet and Spicy Maple Glazed Acorn Squash 131
- Parmesan Zucchini Chips 132

DESSERTS AND SWEET TREATS 133
- Air Fryer Donuts 133
- Apple Pie Egg Rolls 134
- Chocolate Chip Cookies 135
- Banana Fritters 136
- Air Fryer Churros 137
- Strawberry Shortcake Biscuits: 138
- Pineapple Upside-Down Cake 139
- S'mores Crescent Rolls: 140
- Air Fryer Brownies 141
- Cinnamon Sugar Pretzel Bites 142

CONCLUTION 143
FREQUENTLY QUESTION 144
GLOSSARY 148

INTRODUCTION

Greetings from the realm of air fryers! This cookbook, The Complete Air Fryer Recipes Cookbook, takes us on a culinary adventure that will completely change the way we prepare and consume our favorite foods. With no taste or texture loss, air frying is a healthier alternative to standard frying techniques that is quickly gaining traction in kitchens throughout the globe. This cookbook is the best resource for realizing the full potential of this adaptable kitchen tool, regardless of experience level or level of interest in air frying.

The idea of air-frying is simple yet very powerful. With a fraction of the oil needed in conventional frying techniques, an air fryer produces beautifully crispy and golden-brown foods by rapidly circulating hot air over the food to create an exterior layer of crispiness while maintaining moisture inside. It's possible to make everything from crispy chicken wings to flawlessly roasted veggies, and the results are always amazing.

This cookbook has a wide range of recipes that have been thoughtfully chosen to highlight the air fryer's flexibility. Everything from traditional breakfast fare to delicious appetizers, filling main courses, and decadent desserts is sure to please. Each recipe is meant to be accessible and simple to follow, with clear directions, helpful hints, and eye-catching pictures, so you can be certain that every meal you make turns out well.

However, this cookbook is a celebration of taste, inventiveness, and the love of cooking rather than merely a list of recipes. It's about creating new culinary favorites, reimagining traditional recipes, and spending special meals with those you care about. The recipes in this cookbook are guaranteed to wow and please, whether you're preparing food for your family, yourself, or a gathering of friends.

In addition to dishes, this cookbook provides insightful information on the world of air fryers. Learn about the advantages of air fryer cooking, as well as practical suggestions for operating it efficiently and safety precautions to guarantee a flawless cooking experience. You'll also discover tips for converting recipes, changing ingredients, and resolving frequent problems, giving you the confidence and ease to get the most out of your air fryer.

I want to encourage you to embrace creativity, exploration, and the excitement of discovery as you set out on your air fryer journey. It's okay to modify recipes to your preferences or experiment with other flavor combinations. Let this cookbook be your go-to source for inspiration while cooking, whether you're making a fast weekday supper or a big meal for a celebration. It will motivate you to produce tasty, healthful foods that feed your body and spirit.

Prepare for a unique culinary adventure by preheating your air fryer, gathering your ingredients, and getting set to cook. In the realm of air frying, there's always something new to learn, regardless of experience level. So let's get started and examine all of the options. Have fun in the kitchen!

BENEFITS OF AIR FRYING

Healthier Cooking: One of the biggest advantages of air frying is that, in comparison to conventional frying techniques, it uses a lot less oil to create tasty, crispy food. Food is cooked using hot air circulation in air fryers, which require very little oil to produce a crispy finish. By consuming less oil, you may cut calories and minimize your chance of developing health issues like obesity, heart disease, and high cholesterol that are linked to high-fat diets.

Decreased Fat Level: Air frying considerably lowers the fat level of fried dishes by using little or no oil. Deep-fried food traditionally absorbs a lot of fat from the oil it is submerged in, adding to the dish's total caloric load. Air-frying produces lighter, healthier meals without compromising flavor or texture because it lets excess fat escape from the food as it cooks.

Less Odor and Mess: Since air frying doesn't need a lot of heated oil, it requires less cleaning and mess than conventional frying techniques. Air frying is a cleaner, more convenient cooking method since it leaves no oily residue or fried food odor in the kitchen. To make cleaning even simpler, many air fryer models come with dishwasher-safe parts.

Versatility: Air fryers are very adaptable kitchen tools that work well for cooking a broad range of dishes, including tender meats and vegetables as well as crunchy appetizers and snacks. They are useful for a variety of culinary chores since they can bake, grill, roast, and even reheat leftovers. Air fryers provide versatility and accuracy to produce flawless results every time, thanks to their changeable temperature settings and cooking presets.

Faster Cooking Time: Because air fryers use intense hot air circulation to cook food fast and evenly, they usually need shorter cooking periods than conventional techniques. This may be especially helpful for families or busy people who want to cook more quickly without compromising on quality or flavor. You can prepare delectable meals faster with air frying, whether you're throwing a last-minute party or making a quick supper for your family.

Crispy Texture: Similar to deep-frying, air-frying results in food with a crispy, golden-brown surface and a tender inside. Hot air in circulation produces a convection effect that seals in moisture and crisps the food's exterior layer, giving it a pleasant crunch without using too much oil or fat. Air frying creates the ideal texture and taste combination for a variety of foods, including onion rings, fish fillets, and chicken wings and fries.

All things considered, air frying provides a hassle-free, healthier alternative to conventional frying techniques, letting you enjoy your favorite fried dishes guilt-free. An air fryer may be a useful tool to have in your kitchen, whether your goal is to save weight, expedite your cooking, or just enjoy crispy delicacies without the added calories. The way you cook and eat will be completely changed for years to come by air frying because of its adaptability, quickness, and health advantages.

TIPS FOR USING AN AIR FRYER

As with conventional ovens, preheating your air fryer may assist in guaranteeing that your food cooks through and crisps up correctly. Before adding your ingredients, the majority of air fryers include a preheat feature or need to be preheated for a few minutes.

Use Oil Sparingly: Compared to conventional frying techniques, air frying uses a lot less oil, yet even a little bit of oil may improve the taste and texture of your meal. Before cooking, gently cover your ingredients with oil using a brush or spray bottle. As an alternative, you may disperse oil evenly and sparingly by using cooking spray.

Don't Overcrowd the Basket: Keep your food in the air fryer basket for just the right amount of space so that it cooks evenly and crisps up. To ensure enough air circulation, arrange your components in a single layer, allowing some space between each piece. Cook in batches if needed to prevent crowding.

Flip or Shake Midway Through Cooking: To get the best results, turn or shake your meal midway through cooking. This keeps everything from sticking together and promotes even cooking. To gently shake or turn the food, use tongs or a spatula, being cautious not to scuff the breading or coating.

Modify the Temperature and Cooking Time: When using an air fryer, various dishes call for varied cooking periods and temperatures. For suggested settings, consult recipes or cooking instructions; however, feel free to modify the temperature and cooking time according to your tastes and the particulars of your air fryer. As your meal cooks, keep an eye on it and modify it as necessary.

Use Parchment Paper or Aluminum Foil: You may line the air fryer basket with parchment paper or aluminum foil to prevent food from sticking and to facilitate cleaning. To ensure enough air circulation, use foil or parchment paper that has been perforated. This is particularly useful for preparing meals that include batters or marinades that adhere to the food.

Try Different Spices and Flavors: Adding personal touches to your food's taste with a variety of spices, marinades, and coatings is one of the best things about air frying. Take your time experimenting with sauces, rubs, herbs, and spices to improve the flavor of your favorite dishes.

Check for Doneness: To make sure that meat, poultry, and fish are cooked to the right degree and safe to consume, use a food thermometer to measure their interior temperature. Furthermore, make sure the outside of your dish is crispy and golden brown by physically inspecting it.

Let It Rest: To let the flavors meld and the extra moisture escape, let your cooked dish sit for a few minutes before serving. By doing this, you can make sure that the interior of your dish is moist and the exterior is crispy.

Clean and Maintain Frequently: As directed by the manufacturer, give your air fryer a thorough cleaning after every use. Wipe off the inside and outside of the air fryer with a moist towel after removing and cleaning the basket, tray, and any other detachable pieces in warm, soapy water. Your air fryer will operate at its best and last longer with regular maintenance.

Read the Instruction handbook: Ensure you have thoroughly read the manufacturer's instruction handbook before using your air fryer for the first time. To guarantee safe and appropriate operation, familiarize yourself with the features, operations, and safety instructions of the appliance.

Place on a solid Surface: To avoid your air fryer toppling over while in use, set it down on a level, solid surface. Steer clear of positioning it close to counters or other surfaces where an unintentional knock might occur.

Provide Enough Room for Adequate Air Circulation: Make sure that the air fryer has enough room around it for appropriate ventilation and air circulation. Stay away from positioning it next to cupboards, walls, or other appliances that can impede ventilation and result in overheating.

Use on Heat-Resistant Surfaces: To prevent heat damage to your tables or counters, place your air fryer on a heat-resistant surface like a trivet or mat. Keep it away from heat-sensitive surfaces like plastic or wooden counters.

Keep Away from Water: To avoid electrical shock and damage, air fryers should be kept away from water and other liquids as they are electrical appliances. Avoid submerging the air fryer in water or using water to clean it while it's connected.

Wear Oven Mitts or Heat-Resistant Gloves: To prevent burns and other damage to your hands, wear oven mitts or heat-resistant gloves while handling the air fryer basket or tray during or after cooking. During operation, the basket and tray may become very hot, and they may continue to be hot after cooking.

Refrain from Overfilling the Basket: Don't put too much food in the air fryer basket to avoid spilling oil and to guarantee uniform cooking. For maximum fill levels, according to the manufacturer's instructions and, if needed, cook in batches.

Avoid Using Metal Utensils: To prevent scratches on the non-stick coating and damage to the air fryer, do not use metal utensils or abrasive cleaning equipment inside the device. As an alternative, use plastic, silicone, or wooden utensils to prevent harm to the tray or basket.

Watch the Cooking Process: To avoid overcooking or burning, keep a watch on your food while it cooks in the air fryer. Depending on the particular recipe and your tastes, adjust the cooking time and temperature as necessary.

When Not in Use: Unplug the air fryer from the power socket after using it to avoid inadvertent activation and to save electricity. Before cleaning and putting the equipment away, let it cool fully.

You may use your air fryer with confidence and peace of mind if you adhere to these safety instructions since you will be taking the required safety measures to avoid mishaps and injuries. Happy and secure cooking!

BREAKFAST DELIGHTS

Air Fryer Breakfast Burritos

Prep Time: 15 minutes | **Cooking Time**: 10 minutes | **Total Time**: 25 minutes | **Servings**: 4

Ingredients:

- 4 large flour tortillas
- 1/2 cup cooked breakfast sausage (chorizo, bacon, or ham)
- 1/2 cup scrambled eggs
- 1/2 cup shredded cheddar cheese
- 1/4 cup diced red bell pepper
- 1/4 cup diced green onion
- 1/4 cup chopped fresh cilantro
- Salt and pepper to taste
- Avocado oil cooking spray

Directions:

1. Preheat your air fryer to 400°F (200°C).
2. Assemble the burritos: Lay out a tortilla on a flat surface. Divide the cooked sausage, scrambled eggs, cheese, bell pepper, green onion, and cilantro evenly among the tortillas. Season with salt and pepper to taste.
3. Fold the burritos: Fold the bottom third of the tortilla up over the filling. Then, fold in the sides of the tortilla, creating an envelope shape. Roll the tortilla tightly to enclose the filling.
4. Lightly spray the burritos with avocado oil cooking spray.
5. Air fry the burritos: Place the burritos seam-side down in the preheated air fryer basket. Cook for 5-7 minutes, or until golden brown and crispy. Be sure not to overcrowd the basket, cook in batches if necessary.
6. Serve immediately with your favorite salsa, hot sauce, avocado slices, or sour cream.

Nutritional Information per serving: Calories: 350, Fat: 15g, Saturated Fat: 5g, Cholesterol: 200mg, , Sodium: 400mg, Carbohydrates: 30g, Fiber: 5g, Sugar: 5, Protein: 20g

Tips:

- You can use pre-cooked sausage or bacon to save time.
- Add other vegetables to your liking, such as diced potatoes, chopped spinach, or black beans.
- Substitute cheese with other varieties like swiss, pepper jack, or queso fresco.
- To make these burritos ahead of time, assemble them and wrap them tightly in plastic wrap. Refrigerate for up to 2 days or freeze for up to 3 months. Reheat in the air fryer at 350°F (175°C) for 5-7 minutes, or until heated through.
- For a vegetarian option, replace the sausage with cooked black beans or tofu scramble.

Crispy Hash Brown Patties

Prep Time: 10 minutes | **Cook Time**: 12-15 minutes | **Total Time**: 25-30 minutes | **Servings**: 2

Ingredients:

- 2 medium russet potatoes (about 12 ounces)
- 1/4 cup finely chopped onion (optional)
- 1 tablespoon melted butter or olive oil
- powder (optional)
- 1/2 teaspoon salt
- 1/4 teaspoon black pepper
- 1/4 teaspoon garlic powder (optional)
- 1/4 teaspoon onion

Directions:

1. Preheat: Preheat your air fryer to 400°F (200°C). Lightly grease the basket with cooking spray or a mist of oil.
2. Shred Potatoes: Wash and peel the potatoes. Using a box grater with the large holes, shred the potatoes into a large bowl. If using frozen hash browns, skip this step.
3. Squeeze Out Excess Moisture: Place the shredded potatoes in a clean dish towel or cheesecloth and squeeze out as much excess moisture as possible. This is crucial for achieving crispy hash browns.
4. Add Flavorings: In the bowl with the potatoes, add the chopped onion (if using), melted butter or oil, salt, pepper, garlic powder, and onion powder (if using). Mix well to combine.
5. Form Patties: Using your hands, gently form the potato mixture into 4 equal-sized patties. Be careful not to overwork the mixture, as this can make the hash browns tough.
6. Air Fry!: Place the hash brown patties in a single layer in the preheated air fryer basket. Do not overcrowd the basket, as this will prevent even cooking.
7. Cook & Flip: Cook for 12-15 minutes, or until golden brown and crispy on the outside, and cooked through on the inside. Flip the patties halfway through cooking for even browning.
8. Serve & Enjoy!: Plate your crispy hash brown patties and enjoy them immediately with your favorite breakfast dishes or dipping sauce.

Nutritional Information per serving: Calories: 220, Fat: 6g, Carbohydrates: 28g, Fiber: 2g, Protein: 4g, Sodium: 200mg

Tips:

- For extra crispy hash browns, use Yukon Gold potatoes instead of russet potatoes.
- For a cheesy twist, sprinkle shredded cheddar cheese on top of the patties after flipping them.
- If you don't have an air fryer, you can bake the hash browns in a preheated oven at 400°F (200°C) for 20-25 minutes, flipping them halfway through.
- Leftover hash browns can be stored in an airtight container in the refrigerator for up to 3 days. Reheat them in the air fryer or oven until warmed through.

Air Fried French Toast Sticks

Cooking Time: 6-8 minutes, **Prep Time**: 5 minutes, **Total Time**: 11-13 minutes, **Serving Size**: 4-6

Ingredients:

- 4 slices thick bread (Brioche, Texas toast, or Challah work well)
- 2 large eggs
- 1/3 cup milk (dairy or non-dairy)
- 1 teaspoon vanilla extract
- 1/2 teaspoon ground cinnamon
- 1/4 teaspoon ground nutmeg (optional)
- Pinch of salt
- Cooking spray
- Powdered sugar, maple syrup, fresh fruit (for serving)

Directions:

1. Prep: Cut the bread slices into thirds lengthwise, creating French toast sticks. Whisk together eggs, milk, vanilla extract, cinnamon, nutmeg (if using), and salt in a shallow dish.
2. Preheat: Preheat your air fryer to 375°F (190°C) for 3 minutes. Lightly coat the basket with cooking spray.
3. Dip and Coat: Working in batches, dip each bread stick into the egg mixture, ensuring thorough coating. Allow excess drips to fall back into the dish before placing the stick in the air fryer basket. Arrange the sticks in a single layer, avoiding overcrowding.
4. Air Fry: Cook for 5-6 minutes per batch, flipping halfway through for even browning. If using thicker bread, adjust cooking time accordingly. Watch closely to avoid burning.
5. Serve: Transfer the cooked sticks to a plate. Repeat with remaining batches. Dust with powdered sugar, drizzle with maple syrup, and top with fresh fruit for a decadent finish.

Nutritional Information per serving Calories: 200, Fat: 5g, Saturated Fat: 2g, Cholesterol: 75mg, Sodium: 150mg, Carbohydrates: 25g, Sugar: 5g, Fiber: 2g, Protein: 6g

Tips:

- Use slightly stale bread for better absorption of the custard mixture.
- Add a tablespoon of melted butter to the egg mixture for richer flavor.
- Experiment with different spices like pumpkin spice or cardamom for a flavor twist.
- Double the recipe to feed a crowd or freeze leftover cooked sticks for another quick breakfast.
- Enjoy your crispy, guilt-free Air Fried French Toast Sticks!

Breakfast Sausage Links or Patties

Prep Time: 5 minutes | **Total Time**: 12-15 minutes | **Servings**: 2-3

Ingredients:

For both Links and Patties:
- 1 package (12oz) breakfast sausage links or patties (turkey, pork, chicken, etc.)
- Olive oil spray (optional)

Directions:

Crispy Sausage Links:

1. Preheat your Air Fryer to 400°F (200°C).
2. Pat the sausage links dry with paper towels. This helps achieve a crispier exterior.
3. Lightly spray the air fryer basket with olive oil, if desired. This is optional, but helps prevent sticking.
4. Arrange the sausage links in a single layer in the basket. Avoid overcrowding, as this can lead to uneven cooking.
5. Air fry for 8-10 minutes, flipping halfway through. Cook until golden brown and cooked through (internal temperature of 160°F).
6. Serve immediately! Enjoy plain, dipped in your favorite sauce, or added to your breakfast dish.
7. Juicy Sausage Pattie
8. Follow steps 1-3 from the Links recipe.
9. Air fry for 10-12 minutes, flipping halfway through. Cook until cooked through (internal temperature of 160°F).
10. Serve immediately! These patties are perfect for breakfast sandwiches or crumbled into scrambles.

Nutritional Information per serving: Calories: 250-300, Fat: 20-25g, Protein: 20-25g, Carbs: 0-5g

Tips:

- For frozen sausage, add 2-3 minutes to the cooking time.
- You can adjust the cooking time slightly based on your desired level of crispness.
- Feel free to experiment with different seasonings! Sprinkle your sausage with paprika, cayenne pepper, or your favorite herbs before air frying.
- Leftover cooked sausage can be stored in an airtight container in the refrigerator for up to 3 days. Reheat in the air fryer or microwave until warmed through.
- No matter which shape you choose, your Air Fryer will deliver perfectly cooked, delicious breakfast sausage in no time!

Air Fryer Breakfast Potatoes with Peppers and Onions

Cook Time: 15-20 minutes | **Prep Time**: 10 minutes | **Total Time**: 25-30 minutes | **Serving Size**: 2-3 servings

Ingredients:

- 2 medium potatoes (russet or Yukon gold), diced into ½-inch cubes
- 1 bell pepper (any color), diced
- ½ medium onion, diced
- 2 tablespoons olive oil
- 1 teaspoon garlic powder
- ½ teaspoon onion powder
- ½ teaspoon smoked paprika
- ¼ teaspoon dried thyme
- Salt and pepper to taste
- Optional: Chopped fresh parsley for garnish

Directions:

1. Preheat your air fryer to 400°F (200°C).
2. In a large bowl, combine the diced potatoes, bell pepper, onion, olive oil, garlic powder, onion powder, smoked paprika, dried thyme, salt, and pepper. Toss well to ensure everything is evenly coated.
3. Arrange the potato mixture in a single layer in your air fryer basket. Avoid overcrowding, as this can lead to uneven cooking.
4. Air fry for 15-20 minutes, shaking the basket halfway through. This ensures even browning and crisping.
5. Check for doneness. The potatoes should be tender on the inside and crispy on the outside. If needed, cook for a few additional minutes.
6. Transfer the potatoes to a serving plate and garnish with chopped fresh parsley, if desired.
7. Serve immediately and enjoy

Nutritional Information per serving: Calories: 200, Fat: 8g, Carbs: 25g, Protein: 3g

Tips:

- For an extra crispy result, soak the diced potatoes in cold water for 10 minutes before drying them thoroughly.
- Feel free to experiment with different seasonings! Try adding cayenne pepper for a kick, cumin for a smoky flavor, or Italian seasoning for a classic herb blend.
- Leftovers can be stored in an airtight container in the refrigerator for up to 3 days. Reheat in the air fryer or oven until crispy again.
- Cinnamon Sugar Donut Holes

Air Fryer Cinnamon Sugar Donut Holes

Cooking Time: 5-7 minutes per batch | **Prep Time**: 15 minutes | **Total Time**: 20-25 minutes | **Serving Size: Approximately** 15-20 donut holes

Ingredients:

- 1 1/2 cups all-purpose flour
- 2 teaspoons baking powder
- 1/2 teaspoon salt
- 1/4 teaspoon ground nutmeg
- 1/4 teaspoon ground cinnamon
- 1/3 cup granulated sugar
- cinnamon
- 1 large egg
- 1/2 cup milk
- 2 tablespoons melted butter
- Vegetable oil spray
- 1/4 cup granulated sugar
- 1 tablespoon ground

Directions:

1. Prepare the dough: In a large bowl, whisk together flour, baking powder, salt, nutmeg, and cinnamon. In a separate bowl, whisk together sugar, egg, milk, and melted butter until combined.
2. Combine wet and dry ingredients: Gradually add the wet ingredients to the dry ingredients, mixing until just combined. Do not over mix. The dough will be slightly sticky.
3. Shape the donut holes: Lightly flour a work surface. With damp hands, pinch off small pieces of dough and roll them into balls about 1-inch in diameter.
4. Preheat the air fryer: Preheat your air fryer to 325°F (163°C). Lightly spray the basket with vegetable oil spray.
5. Cook the donut holes: Working in batches, place the donut holes in a single layer in the preheated air fryer basket. Do not overcrowd the basket. Air fry for 5-7 minutes, or until golden brown and cooked through. Flip the donut holes halfway through cooking for even browning.
6. Make the cinnamon sugar coating: While the donut holes are cooking, combine the 1/4 cup sugar and 1 tablespoon cinnamon in a shallow dish.
7. Coat the donut holes: Once cooked, remove the donut holes from the air fryer and immediately dip them in the melted butter, letting excess drip off. Then, roll them in the cinnamon sugar mixture to coat evenly.
8. Serve warm: Enjoy your air-fried cinnamon sugar donut holes warm and fresh!

Nutritional Information per serving: Calories: 150, Fat: 8g, Saturated Fat: 4g, Carbohydrates: 18g, Sugar: 8g, Protein: 2g, Sodium: 130mg

Tips:

- If your dough is too sticky, add a little more flour, 1 tablespoon at a time, until it becomes manageable.
- Don't overcrowd the air fryer basket, as this can prevent the donut holes from cooking evenly.
- You can adjust the cooking time depending on the size of your donut holes.
- For a fun twist, try dipping the donut holes in melted chocolate or glaze instead of the cinnamon sugar mixture.
- Store leftover donut holes in an airtight container at room temperature for up to 2 days.

Blueberry Muffins with Streusel Topping

Cooking Time: 15 minutes | **Prep Time**: 5 minutes | **Total Time**: 20 minutes | **Serving Size**: 6 muffins

Ingredients:

For the muffins:
- 1 1/2 cups all-purpose flour
- 1/2 cup granulated sugar
- 2 teaspoons baking powder
- 1/4 teaspoon salt
- 1/2 cup milk (whole or 2% recommended)
- 1/4 cup melted butter, cooled
- 1 large egg
- 1 teaspoon vanilla extract
- 1 cup fresh or frozen blueberries

For the streusel topping:
- 1/4 cup all-purpose flour
- 1/4 cup brown sugar
- 1/4 teaspoon ground cinnamon
- 2 tablespoons cold unsalted butter, cubed

Instructions:

1. Preheat your air fryer to 375°F (190°C). Lightly grease a 6-cup muffin pan or use paper liners.
2. Combine dry ingredients: In a medium bowl, whisk together flour, sugar, baking powder, and salt.
3. Make the wet batter: In a separate bowl, whisk together milk, melted butter, egg, and vanilla extract.
4. Combine wet and dry ingredients: Gently fold the wet ingredients into the dry ingredients until just combined. Do not over mix.
5. Gently fold in blueberries: Add the blueberries to the batter and stir with a spatula just until incorporated.
6. Prepare the streusel topping: In a small bowl, combine flour, brown sugar, cinnamon, and cubed butter using a fork or pastry cutter until a crumbly mixture forms.
7. Fill the muffin cups: Divide the batter evenly among the prepared muffin cups. Sprinkle each muffin with the streusel topping.
8. Air fry the muffins: Place the muffin pan in the preheated air fryer and cook for 15 minutes, or until a toothpick inserted into the center of a muffin comes out clean.
9. Cool and serve: Let the muffins cool in the air fryer for a few minutes before transferring them to a wire rack to cool completely. Enjoy warm or at room temperature.

Nutritional Information per muffin: Calories: 220, Fat: 8g, Saturated Fat: 5g, Cholesterol: 35mg, Sodium: 180mg, Carbohydrates: 32g, Fiber: 2g, Sugar: 14g, Protein: 4g

Tips:

- Use ripe but firm blueberries for best results. Frozen blueberries can be used without thawing.
- If your air fryer tends to run hot, reduce the cooking time by 1-2 minutes.
- For a richer flavor, use brown sugar in the muffin batter instead of granulated sugar.
- Add a sprinkle of lemon zest to the streusel topping for a bright citrus flavor.
- Store leftover muffins in an airtight container at room temperature for up to 2 days or in the refrigerator for up to 4 days.

Bacon and Egg Breakfast Pockets

Cooking Time: 10-12 minutes | **Prep Time:** 10 minutes | **Total Time:** 20-22 minutes | **Serving Size:** 4 pockets

Ingredients:
- 1 sheet frozen puff pastry, thawed
- 4 slices bacon, cooked and crumbled
- 4 eggs, beaten
- 1/2 cup shredded cheddar cheese
- 1/4 cup chopped green onions (optional)
- Salt and pepper to taste
- 1 tablespoon milk (for egg wash)

Directions:

1. Preheat your air fryer to 400°F (200°C).
2. Roll out the puff pastry sheet on a lightly floured surface. Cut into 4 equal squares.
3. In a small bowl, whisk together the eggs, salt, and pepper.
4. Divide the cooked bacon, scrambled egg mixture, cheese, and green onions (if using) evenly among the puff pastry squares.
5. Fold each square diagonally into triangles, gently pressing the edges to seal.
6. Whisk the milk in a small bowl to create an egg wash. Brush the tops and sides of each pocket with the egg wash.
7. Arrange the pockets in a single layer in your air fryer basket. Do not overcrowd.
8. Air fry for 10-12 minutes, or until golden brown and the filling is cooked through.
9. Let cool slightly before serving. Enjoy warm!

Nutritional Information Per serving: Calories: 350, Fat: 20g, Protein: 15g, Carbohydrates: 25g

Tips:

- For a richer flavor, brush the inside of each pocket with melted butter before adding the filling.
- Get creative with the cheese! Try using mozzarella, Swiss, or pepper jack for a different flavor profile.
- Add other chopped vegetables to the filling, such as bell peppers, spinach, or mushrooms.
- If you don't have an air fryer, you can bake these pockets in a preheated oven at 400°F (200°C) for 15-20 minutes, or until golden brown and cooked through.
- These pockets can be made ahead of time and frozen for a quick and easy breakfast on busy mornings. Just reheat them in the air fryer for a few minutes until warmed through.

Banana Pancake Bites

Prep Time: 10 minutes | **Cook Time**: 8-10 minutes | **Total Time**: 20 minutes | **Servings:** 2-3 (around 15-20 bites)

Ingredients:

- 1 ripe banana, mashed
- 1/2 cup all-purpose flour
- 1/4 cup milk
- 1 egg
- 1 tablespoon melted butter
- 1/2 teaspoon baking powder
- 1/4 teaspoon baking soda
- 1/4 teaspoon ground cinnamon
- Pinch of salt

Directions:

1. Preheat your air fryer to 350°F (175°C). If using silicone muffin liners, lightly grease them with cooking spray.
2. In a large bowl, mash the banana until smooth.
3. Whisk in the milk, egg, and melted butter until well combined.
4. In a separate bowl, whisk together the flour, baking powder, baking soda, cinnamon, and salt.
5. Gradually add the dry ingredients to the wet ingredients, mixing until just combined. Do not over mix.
6. Spoon the batter into the prepared muffin liners, filling them about ¾ full.
7. Air fry for 8-10 minutes, or until golden brown and cooked through. Flip the bites halfway through cooking if desired, for even browning.
8. Let the bites cool slightly before serving. Top with your favorite toppings and enjoy!

Nutritional Information per serving: Calories: 150-200, Fat: 5g, Saturated Fat: 2g, Carbohydrates: 25g, Sugar: 10g, Protein: 3g, Fiber: 1g,

Tips:

- For a thicker batter, use half mashed banana and half mashed sweet potato.
- Add a handful of chopped nuts or chocolate chips to the batter for extra flavor and texture.
- Serve these warm with a drizzle of maple syrup, honey, or your favorite fruit sauce.
- Leftover bites can be stored in an airtight container in the refrigerator for up to 3 days. Reheat in the air fryer or microwave before serving.
- You can also freeze cooked bites for longer storage. Simply thaw them at room temperature or in the microwave before reheating.

Veggie Breakfast Quesadillas

Cooking Time: 8 minutes | **Prep Time:** 5 minutes | **Total Time:** 13 minutes | **Servings:** 2

Ingredients:

- 2 large flour tortillas
- 2 large eggs
- 1/4 cup chopped bell pepper (any color)
- 1/4 cup chopped onion
- 1/4 cup chopped mushrooms
- 1/4 cup shredded spinach
- 1/4 cup crumbled feta cheese
- 1 tablespoon chopped fresh cilantro
- 1/2 teaspoon chili powder
- 1/4 teaspoon garlic powder
- Salt and pepper to taste

Directions:

1. Prep the Vegetables: Dice the bell pepper, onion, and mushrooms. Roughly chop the spinach.
2. Scramble the Eggs: In a small bowl, whisk the eggs with the chili powder, garlic powder, salt, and pepper. Set aside.
3. Assemble the Quesadillas: Place one tortilla in the air fryer basket. Sprinkle with half of the feta cheese, followed by the chopped vegetables and spinach. Pour half of the scrambled egg mixture over the top.
4. Cook in the Air Fryer: Preheat the air fryer to 375°F (190°C) for 2 minutes. Carefully fold the other tortilla over the filling and cook for 4-5 minutes, or until golden brown and crispy. Repeat with the remaining tortilla and filling.
5. Serve: Slice the quesadillas into wedges and top with additional feta cheese, cilantro, and your favorite hot sauce, if desired.

Nutritional Information: Calories: 350, Fat: 15g, Protein: 18g, Carbohydrates: 25g, Fiber: 4g, Sodium: 300mg

Tips:

- For a richer flavor, add a tablespoon of olive oil or melted butter to the vegetables when cooking.
- If you don't have any spinach, you can substitute it with another leafy green like kale or swiss chard.
- Get creative with the fillings! Try adding other vegetables like avocado, black beans, or corn.
- Leftovers can be stored in an airtight container in the refrigerator for up to 2 days. Reheat in the air fryer or oven until warmed through.

Breakfast Egg Rolls with Sausage and Cheese

Prep Time: 15 minutes | **Cooking Time**: 10 minutes | **Total Time**: 25 minutes | **Servings**: 4

Ingredients:

1 tablespoon olive oil
1/2 pound breakfast sausage, cooked and crumbled
1/2 cup diced bell pepper (any color)
1/4 cup chopped onion
4 large eggs, beaten
1/2 cup shredded cheddar cheese
1/4 cup crumbled feta cheese
1/4 cup chopped fresh chives
Salt and pepper to taste
10 egg roll wrappers

Directions:

1. Preheat your air fryer to 400°F (200°C).
2. In a large skillet, heat olive oil over medium heat. Add the sausage, bell pepper, and onion. Cook until the sausage is browned and the vegetables are softened, about 5 minutes.
3. In a separate bowl, whisk together the eggs, cheddar cheese, feta cheese, and chives. Season with salt and pepper to taste.
4. Lay out an egg roll wrapper with one corner facing you. Place about 2 tablespoons of the sausage mixture and 1 tablespoon of the egg mixture in the center of the wrapper.
5. Fold the bottom corner of the wrapper up over the filling, then fold in the sides. Roll up tightly, tucking in the ends as you go. Brush the outside of the roll with water.
6. Repeat steps 4-5 with the remaining wrappers and filling.
7. Arrange the egg rolls in a single layer in the air fryer basket, ensuring they don't touch. Spray lightly with cooking oil.
8. Cook for 8-10 minutes, or until golden brown and crispy. Flip the egg rolls halfway through cooking for even browning.
9. Serve immediately with your favorite dipping sauce, such as hot sauce, salsa, or ketchup.

Nutritional Information per serving: Calories: 350, Protein: 15g, Fat: 20g, Carbohydrates: 15g, Sodium: 400mg

Tips:

- For a vegetarian option, replace the sausage with crumbled tofu or tempeh.
- Add other vegetables to the filling, such as mushrooms, spinach, or broccoli.
- If you don't have an air fryer, you can bake the egg rolls in a preheated oven at 400°F (200°C) for 15-20 minutes, or until golden brown and crispy.
- Prepare the filling ahead of time and store it in the refrigerator overnight for easy assembly in the morning.
- Make sure your egg rolls are not touching in the air fryer basket for even cooking and crisping.

Apple Cinnamon Roll-Ups

Prep Time: 10 minute | **Cook Time**: 8-10 minutes | **Total Time**: 20 minutes | **Servings**: 4

Ingredients:

- 1 sheet refrigerated crescent dough, unrolled
- 1 tablespoon melted butter
- 1/4 cup packed light brown sugar
- 1 teaspoon ground cinnamon
- 1 apple, peeled, cored, and thinly sliced
- 1/4 cup powdered sugar
- 1 tablespoon milk
- Optional toppings: Chopped nuts, raisins, maple syrup

Instructions:

1. Preheat your air fryer to 375°F (190°C).
2. In a small bowl, combine the brown sugar and cinnamon. Spread the melted butter evenly over the crescent dough sheet. Sprinkle the cinnamon-sugar mixture over the butter.
3. Arrange the apple slices evenly over the dough. Starting at one long end, roll up the dough tightly, pinching the seams to seal.
4. Use a sharp knife to cut the roll-up into 8 equal pieces. Place the pieces in your air fryer basket, leaving a little space between them.
5. Air fry for 8-10 minutes, or until golden brown and cooked through.
6. While the roll-ups are cooking, whisk together the powdered sugar and milk in a small bowl until smooth.
7. Once cooked, remove the roll-ups from the air fryer and let them cool slightly. Drizzle with the icing and sprinkle with your desired toppings, if using.

Nutritional Information per Serving: Calories: 250, Fat: 8g, Saturated Fat: 4g, Sugar: 15g, Carbohydrates: 35g, Fiber: 2g, Protein: 4g

Tips:

- For a richer flavor, use full-fat crescent dough.
- You can substitute other fruits for the apples, such as pears, peaches, or berries.
- If you don't have an air fryer, you can bake the roll-ups at 375°F (190°C) for 15-20 minutes, or until golden brown and cooked through.
- Serve the roll-ups warm with a side of yogurt or fruit salad for a complete breakfast.

Greek Yogurt Parfait with Granola and Berries

Cooking Time: N/A | **Prep Time**: 5 minutes | **Total Time**: 5 minutes | **Serving Size**: 1

Ingredients:

- 1/2 cup plain Greek yogurt (or flavored yogurt of your choice)
- 1/4 cup granola (homemade or store-bought)
- 1/4 cup fresh berries (blueberries, strawberries, raspberries, etc.)
- 1/4 cup chopped fruit (apple, banana, mango, etc.)
- 1 tablespoon honey or maple syrup
- Chopped nuts and seeds (almonds, walnuts, chia seeds, etc.)

Directions:

1. Gather your ingredients. Wash and chop any fresh fruit you're using.
2. Assemble the parfait: In a bowl or jar, layer 1/4 cup of the yogurt. Top with 1/4 cup of the granola.
3. Add fruit: Add 1/4 cup of your chosen fresh berries and 1/4 cup of chopped fruit (if using). Drizzle with honey or maple syrup if desired.
4. Repeat: Repeat layers of yogurt, granola, and fruit until you reach the desired height or until you've used all your ingredients.
5. Finish: Top with a sprinkle of chopped nuts and seeds for added texture and nutrients.
6. Serve immediately and enjoy!

Nutritional Information per serving : Calories: Approximately 300-400, Fat: 5-10g, Carbohydrates: 30-40g, Protein: 15-20g

Tips:

- Use different fruits and flavors of yogurt to create endless variations.
- Make the parfait ahead of time and store it in the refrigerator for a grab-and-go breakfast.
- Substitute granola with rolled oats or muesli for a lower-fat option.
- Add a layer of chia pudding for extra protein and fiber.
- Get creative with the toppings! Use shredded coconut, cacao nibs, or a drizzle of nut butter for added flavor and crunch.

Spinach and Feta Mini Quiches

Cooking Time: 15 minutes | **Prep Time:** 10 minutes | **Total Time:** 25 minutes | **Serving Size:** 12 mini quiches

Ingredients:

- 1 sheet frozen puff pastry, thawed
- 1 tablespoon olive oil
- 1/2 onion, finely diced
- 1 clove garlic, minced
- 4 ounces baby spinach, chopped
- 1/4 cup crumbled feta cheese
- 1/4 cup shredded mozzarella cheese
- 2 large eggs
- 1/4 cup milk
- 1/4 teaspoon dried oregano
- Salt and pepper to taste

Directions:

1. Preheat your air fryer to 375°F (190°C). Lightly grease a mini muffin pan with cooking spray.
2. Cut the puff pastry into 12 equal squares. Gently press each square into the greased muffin cups, forming little bowls.
3. Heat the olive oil in a pan over medium heat. Add the onion and cook until softened, about 3 minutes. Add the garlic and cook for another minute, until fragrant.
4. Stir in the spinach and cook until wilted, about 2 minutes. Remove from the heat and let cool slightly.
5. In a bowl, whisk together the eggs, milk, oregano, salt, and pepper.
6. Divide the spinach mixture and feta cheese evenly among the muffin cups. Top with the mozzarella cheese.
7. Pour the egg mixture evenly over the fillings.
8. Air fry for 15 minutes, or until the quiches are golden brown and set.
9. Let cool for a few minutes before serving.

Nutritional Information per quiche: Calories: 150, Fat: 8g, Protein: 7g, Carbs: 10g, Fiber: 1g,

Tips:

- For a vegetarian option, omit the feta cheese.
- Add other chopped vegetables to the filling, such as mushrooms, bell peppers, or sun-dried tomatoes.
- For a richer flavor, use cream instead of milk in the egg mixture.
- Leftover quiches can be stored in an airtight container in the refrigerator for up to 3 days. Reheat in the air fryer at 350°F (175°C) for a few minutes until warmed through.
- Enjoy your delicious and nutritious Spinach and Feta Mini Quiches!

Air Fried Breakfast Pizza with Eggs and Bacon

Cook Time: 10-12 minutes | **Prep Time**: 5 minutes | **Total Time**: 15-17 minutes | **Servings**: 2

Ingredients:

- 1 pre-made pizza crust (store-bought or homemade)
- 2 eggs
- 2-3 slices cooked bacon, crumbled
- 1/4 cup shredded cheddar cheese
- 1/4 cup shredded mozzarella cheese
- 1/4 cup chopped bell peppers (optional)
- 1/4 cup chopped green onions (optional)
- Salt and pepper to taste
- Cooking spray

Directions:

1. Preheat your air fryer to 375°F (190°C).
2. Place the pizza crust in the air fryer basket and cook for 3-4 minutes, or until the crust is slightly golden brown and crisp.
3. In a bowl, whisk together the eggs. Season with salt and pepper.
4. Carefully remove the crust from the air fryer and pour the whisked eggs evenly over the top.
5. Sprinkle the crumbled bacon, cheddar cheese, and mozzarella cheese over the eggs.
6. (Optional) Top with chopped bell peppers and green onions for added flavor and texture.
7. Return the pizza to the air fryer and cook for an additional 5-7 minutes, or until the eggs are set and the cheese is melted and bubbly.
8. Remove the pizza from the air fryer and let it cool for a few minutes before slicing and serving.

Nutritional Information per serving: Calories: 450, Fat: 25g, Carbs: 30g, Protein: 20g, Sodium: 500mg

Tips:

- Use a pre-cooked bacon crumbles to shorten the prep time.
- Want it spicier? Add a dash of hot sauce to the eggs or sprinkle some red pepper flakes on top.
- Get creative with toppings! Try other cheeses, vegetables, sausage, spinach, or avocado.
- For a thicker crust, pre-bake the dough in the air fryer for 2-3 minutes before adding the toppings.
- Leftovers can be stored in an airtight container in the refrigerator for up to 2 days. Reheat in the air fryer until warmed through.

Stuffed Breakfast Peppers with Eggs and Cheese

Cooking Time: 20 minutes | **Prep Time**: 10 minutes | **Total Time**: 30 minutes | **Serving Size**: 2 servings

Ingredients:

- 2 bell peppers (any color)
- 2 eggs
- 1/4 cup chopped vegetables (onion, bell pepper, spinach, mushroom, etc.)
- 1/4 cup cooked protein (sausage, bacon, ham, tofu, etc.) (optional)
- 1/4 cup shredded cheese (cheddar, mozzarella, pepper jack, etc.)
- 1/4 teaspoon dried herbs (optional, such as basil, oregano, thyme)
- Salt and pepper to taste

Directions:

1. Prep the peppers: Preheat your air fryer to 400°F (200°C). Wash and halve the bell peppers lengthwise, removing the seeds and membranes.
2. Sauté the filling (optional): If using, heat a pan with a little oil over medium heat. Sauté the chopped vegetables and cooked protein until softened and lightly browned. Season with salt and pepper.
3. Assemble the peppers: Divide the sautéed filling (if using) between the pepper halves. Crack an egg into each pepper half.
4. Season and top: Sprinkle the cheese, herbs (if using), salt, and pepper over the eggs.
5. Air fry!: Place the stuffed peppers in the air fryer basket, ensuring they don't touch each other. Air fry for 15-20 minutes, or until the egg whites are set and the cheese is melted and bubbly.
6. Serve and enjoy!: Carefully remove the peppers from the air fryer and let them cool slightly before serving. Enjoy!

Nutritional Information per serving: Calories: 250, Fat: 13g, Carbs: 10g, Protein: 12g, Fiber: 2g

Tips:

- For a spicier kick, add a pinch of red pepper flakes to the filling.
- Get creative with the fillings! Use your favorite breakfast ingredients like diced potatoes, crumbled breakfast sausage, or chopped tomatoes.
- If you don't have an air fryer, you can bake the stuffed peppers in a preheated oven at 400°F (200°C) for 20-25 minutes.
- These peppers can be assembled ahead of time and stored in the fridge overnight. Just air fry them directly from the fridge, adding a few minutes to the cooking time.

Air Fryer Breakfast Bombs filled with Ham, Egg, and Cheese

Prep Time: 15 minutes | **Cook Time**: 10 minutes | **Total Time**: 25 minutes | **Serving Size**: 8

Ingredients:

- 1 can (10.7 oz) refrigerated buttermilk biscuits, separated
- 1 tablespoon olive oil
- 1/4 cup chopped onion (optional)
- 1/4 cup chopped green bell pepper (optional)
- 1/4 cup diced ham
- 2 eggs, beaten
- 1/2 cup shredded cheddar cheese
- Salt and black pepper to taste

Directions:

1. Preheat your air fryer to 375°F (190°C). Lightly grease the basket with cooking spray or olive oil.
2. In a small skillet, heat olive oil over medium heat. Add onion and bell pepper (if using) and cook until softened, about 5 minutes. Stir in the ham and cook for an additional minute.
3. In a separate bowl, combine the beaten eggs, cheese, salt, and pepper. Stir in the cooked ham mixture.
4. Separate the biscuits and gently roll each one out slightly with a rolling pin. Place about 1-2 tablespoons of the filling in the center of each biscuit.
5. Fold the biscuits over the filling, pinching the edges to seal. You can also roll them into balls if desired.
6. Place the breakfast bombs in the preheated air fryer basket, leaving space between them.
7. Air fry for 8-10 minutes, or until golden brown and cooked through. Be sure to flip them halfway through cooking.
8. Serve immediately with your favorite dipping sauce, such as ketchup, hot sauce, or salsa.

Nutritional Information per Serving: Calories: 250, Fat: 12g, Saturated Fat: 5g, Cholesterol: 180mg, Sodium: 350mg, Carbohydrates: 15g, Fiber: 1g, Sugar: 2g, Protein: 15g

Tips:

- For a vegetarian option, omit the ham and add chopped spinach or mushrooms to the filling.
- If you don't have an air fryer, you can bake the breakfast bombs in a preheated oven at 375°F (190°C) for 15-20 minutes, or until golden brown and cooked through.
- You can prepare the filling and assemble the breakfast bombs ahead of time and store them in the refrigerator overnight. Just air fry them as directed when ready to eat.

Strawberry Banana Breakfast Wraps with Nutella

Cooking Time: 5 minutes | **Prep Time**: 5 minutes | **Total Time**: 10 minutes | **Serving Size**: 2 wraps

Ingredients:

- 2 whole wheat tortillas
- 2 tablespoons Nutella
- 1/2 banana, sliced
- 1/4 cup strawberries, sliced
- 1/4 teaspoon ground cinnamon (optional)
- 1 tablespoon chopped walnuts or pecans (optional)

Directions:

1. Prep the Fillings: Slice the banana and strawberries. Sprinkle with cinnamon and chopped nuts, if using.
2. Spread the Nutella: Warm the tortillas in the microwave for 10-15 seconds to make them more pliable. Spread 1 tablespoon of Nutella on each tortilla, leaving a 1/2-inch border around the edge.
3. Assemble the Wraps: Lay half of the banana slices and strawberry slices on top of the Nutella on one side of each tortilla. Fold the tortillas in half, enclosing the filling.
4. Air Fry: Preheat your air fryer to 350°F (175°C). Place the wraps in the air fryer basket, leaving space between them. Air fry for 3-5 minutes, or until the tortillas are golden brown and crispy.
5. Serve: Slice the wraps in half diagonally and enjoy warm!

Nutritional Information: Calories: 380 per wrap, Fat: 14g per wrap, Carbohydrates: 42g per wrap, Protein: 6g per wrap

Tips:

- You can substitute other nut butters for Nutella, such as peanut butter or almond butter.
- Add a drizzle of honey or maple syrup for extra sweetness.
- Use other fruits like blueberries, raspberries, or mango for variety.
- For a richer flavor, add a swirl of whipped cream or ricotta cheese before folding the wraps.
- To make ahead, assemble the wraps and store them in an airtight container in the refrigerator overnight. Air fry them just before serving.

Cranberry Orange Scones with Glaze

Cooking Time: 15 minutes | **Prep Time:** 10 minutes | **Total Time:** 25 minutes | **Serving Size:** 8 scones

Ingredients:

For the Scones:
- 2 cups all-purpose flour
- 3 tablespoons granulated sugar
- 2 teaspoons baking powder
- 1/2 teaspoon salt
- 1/4 teaspoon ground cinnamon (optional)
- 1/2 cup (1 stick) unsalted butter, cold and cubed
- 1/2 cup fresh or frozen cranberries
- 1/2 cup + 1 tablespoon heavy cream, divided
- 1 large egg
- 1 teaspoon vanilla extract
- 1 tablespoon orange zest

For the Glaze:
- 1 cup powdered sugar
- 2-3 tablespoons orange juice

Instructions:

1. Preheat your air fryer to 375°F (190°C). Lightly grease the air fryer basket with cooking spray.
2. In a large bowl, whisk together the flour, sugar, baking powder, salt, and cinnamon (if using). Cut in the cold butter using a pastry cutter or your fingertips until the mixture resembles coarse crumbs.
3. Stir in the cranberries and 1/2 cup of heavy cream. Mix until a dough forms, adding more cream by the tablespoon if needed. Gently fold in the orange zest.
4. Turn the dough out onto a lightly floured surface and gently pat it into a 1-inch thick circle. Cut the circle into 8 wedges.
5. Arrange the scones in the air fryer basket, leaving space between them. Brush the tops with the remaining tablespoon of heavy cream.
6. Air fry for 15-17 minutes, or until golden brown and cooked through.
7. While the scones bake, prepare the glaze. In a small bowl, whisk together the powdered sugar and orange juice until smooth and thin enough to drizzle.
8. Let the scones cool slightly before drizzling with the glaze. Serve warm and enjoy!

Nutritional Information per Scone: Calories: 250, Fat: 12g, Carbs: 30g, Sugar: 15g, Protein: 4g

Tips:

- If you don't have an air fryer, you can bake the scones in a preheated oven at 400°F (200°C) for 18-20 minutes.
- For a richer flavor, use full-fat heavy cream.
- You can substitute dried cranberries for fresh cranberries, but they may be a bit chewier.
- Add a pinch of nutmeg or cardamom to the dough for an extra touch of spice.
- Get creative with the glaze! You can use other citrus juices, such as lemon or grapefruit, or add a splash of almond extract for a different flavor.

Breakfast Tater Tots Casserole with Eggs, Cheese, and Bacon

Cooking Time: 20-25 minutes | **Prep Time**: 10 minutes | **Total Time**: 30-35 minutes | **Servings**: 4-6

Ingredients:

- 1 tablespoon olive oil
- 4 slices bacon, chopped
- 1/2 cup chopped green onion
- 1 (32-oz) bag frozen tater tots
- 8 large eggs
- 1/2 cup milk
- 1/2 cup shredded cheddar cheese
- 1/4 cup shredded Monterey Jack cheese
- 1/4 teaspoon salt
- 1/4 teaspoon black pepper

Directions:

1. Preheat your air fryer to 400°F (200°C).
2. In a small skillet, heat olive oil over medium heat. Add bacon and cook until crispy. Remove with a slotted spoon and set aside.
3. Lightly grease an air fryer-safe baking dish (such as a ceramic dish). Spread half of the tater tots in the bottom of the dish.
4. In a large bowl, whisk together eggs, milk, cheddar cheese, Monterey Jack cheese, salt, and pepper.
5. Pour the egg mixture over the tater tots in the baking dish.
6. Sprinkle the remaining tater tots and cooked bacon on top.
7. Place the baking dish in the air fryer and cook for 20-25 minutes, or until the eggs are set and the tater tots are golden brown and crispy.
8. Garnish with chopped green onion (optional) and serve immediately.

Nutritional Information per serving: Calories: 350, Fat: 20g, Carbs: 30g, Protein: 15g, Sodium: 400mg

Tips:

- Use pre-cooked bacon to save time.
- Add other breakfast favorites like chopped ham, sausage, or bell peppers to the casserole.
- For a richer flavor, use heavy cream instead of milk.
- Leftovers can be stored in an airtight container in the refrigerator for up to 3 days. Reheat in the air fryer at 350°F (175°C) for 5-7 minutes, or until heated through.

LUNCH RECIPES

Crispy Chicken Sandwiches

Cooking Time: 15 minutes | **Prep Time**: 10 minutes | **Total Time**: 25 minutes | **Serving Size**: 2 sandwiches

Ingredients:

- 2 boneless, skinless chicken breasts, pounded thin
- 1/4 cup all-purpose flour
- 1/2 teaspoon garlic powder
- 1/4 teaspoon paprika
- 1/4 teaspoon salt
- 1/4 teaspoon black pepper
- 1 egg, beaten
- 1/2 cup panko breadcrumbs
- 4 slices bacon
- 2 hamburger buns, toasted
- Lettuce, tomato, onion, mayonnaise (optional), your favorite sandwich toppings

Directions:

1. Prep the chicken: In a shallow bowl, combine flour, garlic powder, paprika, salt, and pepper. In another bowl, whisk the egg. In a third bowl, place the panko breadcrumbs. Dredge each chicken breast in the flour mixture, then dip in the egg, and finally coat in the panko breadcrumbs.
2. Cook the bacon: Arrange bacon strips in a single layer in your air fryer basket. Cook at 400°F (200°C) for 5-7 minutes, or until crisp. Transfer to a paper towel-lined plate to drain.
3. Cook the chicken: Preheat your air fryer to 400°F (200°C). Lightly spray the air fryer basket with cooking oil. Place the breaded chicken breasts in the basket, ensuring they don't touch. Cook for 8-10 minutes, flipping halfway through, or until cooked through and golden brown.
4. Assemble the sandwiches: Toast the hamburger buns, if desired. Spread mayonnaise on one side of each bun (optional). Layer lettuce, tomato, onion, cooked chicken, and crispy bacon on one bun. Top with the other bun and enjoy!

Nutritional Information per serving: Calories: 450, Fat: 25g, Carbs: 30g, Protein: 35g, Sodium: 600mg

Tips:

For extra crispy chicken, double dip in the egg and breading mixture.
Use your favorite spices in the flour mixture for added flavor.
Experiment with different cheeses, sauces, and toppings for endless variations.
Leftover chicken can be used in salads, wraps, or other dishes.
For a vegetarian option, replace the chicken with breaded portobello mushrooms or tofu.

Air Fryer Veggie Quesadillas

Prep Time: 10 minutes | **Cooking Time:** 8 minutes | **Total Time:** 18 minutes | **Serving Size:** 2

Ingredients:

- 2 large flour tortillas
- 1 tablespoon olive oil
- 1/2 red bell pepper, diced
- 1/2 green bell pepper, diced
- 1/2 yellow onion, diced
- 1 clove garlic, minced
- 1/2 cup chopped spinach
- 1/4 cup shredded cheddar cheese
- 1/4 cup shredded Monterey Jack cheese
- 1 tablespoon chopped fresh cilantro
- 1/4 teaspoon chili powder
- 1/4 teaspoon cumin
- Salt and pepper to taste

Directions:

1. Preheat your air fryer to 380°F (190°C).
2. Heat the olive oil in a pan over medium heat. Add the bell peppers, onion, and garlic. Cook for 5 minutes, or until softened. Stir in the spinach and cook until wilted.
3. In a bowl, combine the cooked vegetables, cheeses, cilantro, chili powder, cumin, salt, and pepper. Mix well.
4. Place one tortilla in the air fryer basket. Spread half of the vegetable mixture over one half of the tortilla. Fold the tortilla in half to enclose the filling. Repeat with the remaining tortilla and filling.
5. Cook the quesadillas in the air fryer for 4 minutes per side, or until golden brown and crispy.
6. Slice the quesadillas into wedges and serve immediately with your favorite toppings, such as salsa, guacamole, or sour cream.

Nutritional Information per serving: Calories: 350, Fat: 12g, Saturated Fat: 6g, Carbohydrates: 35g, Fiber: 4g, Sugar: 4g, Protein: 15g

Tips:

- Feel free to use any type of vegetables you like in your quesadillas.
- For a spicier quesadilla, add a few dashes of hot sauce to the vegetable mixture.
- You can also add protein to your quesadillas, such as cooked black beans, shredded chicken, or crumbled tofu.
- If your air fryer doesn't have a preheat function, simply cook the quesadillas for an extra minute or two per side.
- Leftover quesadillas can be stored in an airtight container in the refrigerator for up to 3 days. Reheat them in the air fryer for a few minutes before serving.

Buffalo Cauliflower Wraps

Cooking Time: 15 minutes | **Prep Time**: 10 minutes | **Total Time**: 25 minutes | **Serving Size**: 2 wraps

Ingredients:

- 1 head cauliflower, cut into florets
- 1/4 cup all-purpose flour
- 1/2 cup unsweetened plant-based milk
- 1/2 teaspoon paprika
- 1/4 teaspoon garlic powder
- 1/4 teaspoon onion powder
- 1/4 teaspoon black pepper
- 1/2 cup buffalo sauce, plus extra for dipping
- 2 whole wheat tortillas
- Chopped romaine lettuce
- Sliced cucumber
- Shredded carrots
- Crumbled blue cheese (optional)
- Ranch dressing for dipping (optional)

Directions:

1. Prep the Cauliflower: Preheat your air fryer to 400°F (200°C). In a large bowl, whisk together the flour, milk, paprika, garlic powder, onion powder, and black pepper. Add the cauliflower florets and toss until evenly coated.
2. Air Fry the Cauliflower: Arrange the cauliflower florets in a single layer in the air fryer basket. Cook for 10-12 minutes, or until golden brown and crispy, flipping halfway through.
3. Toss in Buffalo Sauce: In a large bowl, toss the cooked cauliflower with the buffalo sauce until evenly coated. You can adjust the amount of sauce to your desired level of spiciness.
4. Assemble the Wraps: Spread a thin layer of buffalo sauce on each tortilla. Top with romaine lettuce, cucumber, carrots, and blue cheese (if using). Divide the buffalo cauliflower florets between the tortillas.
5. Wrap and Enjoy: Fold up the bottom of the tortilla, then fold in the sides. Roll up tightly and enjoy with ranch dressing for dipping (optional).

Nutritional Information per Wrap: Calories: 400, Fat: 15g, Protein: 15g, Carbohydrates: 40g, Fiber: 5g, Sodium: 300mg

Tips:

- For extra crispy cauliflower, use panko breadcrumbs instead of flour in the batter.
- Add cooked shredded chicken or chickpeas for additional protein.
- If you don't have an air fryer, you can roast the cauliflower in a preheated oven at 400°F (200°C) for 20-25 minutes, or until crispy.
- Serve these wraps with a side salad or fruit for a complete and balanced meal.

Turkey Club Wraps:

Prep Time: 10 minutes | **Cooking Time**: 8 minutes | Total Time: 18 minutes | **Servings**: 2

Ingredients:

- 2 large whole-wheat tortillas
- 4 slices cooked turkey breast
- 2 slices cooked bacon, crumbled
- 2 slices cheddar cheese
- 1/4 cup shredded lettuce
- 1 tomato, sliced
- 1/4 avocado, sliced
- 2 tablespoons mayonnaise
- 1 tablespoon Dijon mustard
- Salt and pepper to taste

Directions:

1. Prepare the fillings: In a small bowl, combine mayonnaise, Dijon mustard, salt, and pepper. Spread the mixture evenly on both tortillas.
2. Assemble the wraps: Top each tortilla with turkey, cheese, lettuce, tomato, and avocado.
3. Fold the wraps: Fold the bottom of the tortilla up over the filling, then fold in the sides. Roll the tortilla tightly to enclose the filling. Use toothpicks or skewers to secure the wraps if needed.
4. Air fry the wraps: Preheat your air fryer to 375°F (190°C). Lightly spray the air fryer basket with cooking oil. Place the wraps in the basket, seam-side down, and air fry for 4-5 minutes per side, or until golden brown and crispy.
5. Serve: Remove the wraps from the air fryer and let cool slightly before slicing and serving.

Nutritional Information per serving Calories: 450, Fat: 20g, Saturated Fat: 8g, Carbohydrates: 35g, Sugar: 5g, Protein: 30g

Tips:

- Use rotisserie chicken instead of sliced turkey for a quicker option.
- For a vegetarian version, replace the turkey with sliced tempeh or portobello mushrooms.
- Add other vegetables to your liking, such as cucumbers, red onion, or bell peppers.
- Serve the wraps with a side of ranch dressing or your favorite dipping sauce.
- Leftover wraps can be stored in an airtight container in the refrigerator for up to 2 days. Reheat in the air fryer for a few minutes to crisp them up before serving.

Crispy Tofu Buddha Bowls

Prep Time: 15 minutes | **Cook Time**: 15 minutes | **Total Time**: 30 minutes | **Servings**: 2

Ingredients:

For the Crispy Tofu:
- 14 oz extra-firm tofu, drained and pressed
- 1 tbsp cornstarch
- 1/2 tsp garlic powder
- 1/4 tsp smoked paprika
- Salt and pepper to taste

For the Buddha Bowl:
- 1 cup cooked brown rice or quinoa
- 1 cup roasted or steamed vegetables (e.g., broccoli, carrots, Brussels sprouts)
- 1/2 cup chopped lettuce or spinach
- 1/4 cup sliced avocado
- 1/4 cup cherry tomatoes, halved
- 1/4 cup cooked chickpeas or lentils
- Sesame seeds and fresh herbs for garnish (optional)

For the Sauce (optional):
- 2 tbsp tamari or soy sauce
- 1 tbsp rice vinegar
- 1 tbsp sesame oil
- 1 tsp grated ginger
- 1/2 tsp honey or maple syrup (optional)

Directions:

1. Prepare the Tofu: Preheat your air fryer to 400°F (200°C). Cut the tofu into cubes or slices. In a bowl, toss the tofu with cornstarch, garlic powder, paprika, salt, and pepper.
2. Cook the Tofu: Arrange the tofu in a single layer in the air fryer basket. Depending on the size of your air fryer, you may need to cook in batches. Air fry for 10-12 minutes, flipping halfway, or until golden brown and crispy.
3. Assemble the Bowls: Divide the cooked rice or quinoa among two bowls. Top with roasted vegetables, greens, avocado, tomatoes, chickpeas or lentils, and crispy tofu.
4. Make the Sauce (optional): Whisk together the tamari, rice vinegar, sesame oil, ginger, and honey (if using) in a small bowl. Drizzle the sauce over the bowls to taste.
5. Garnish and Serve: Sprinkle with sesame seeds and fresh herbs (optional) and enjoy!

Nutritional Information per serving: Calories: 450, Fat: 12g, Carbohydrates: 40g, Fiber: 8g, Protein: 25g

Tips:

- For extra crispy tofu, use arrowroot powder instead of cornstarch.
- To save time, use pre-cooked rice or quinoa.
- Get creative with your vegetables! Use what's in season or your personal favorites.
- Add a variety of textures and flavors with different toppings, such as crumbled nuts, seeds, pickled vegetables, or a dollop of hummus.
- This recipe is easily doubled or tripled to feed a crowd.

BBQ Chicken Flatbreads:

Cooking Time: 8 minutes | **Prep Time**: 5 minutes | **Total Time**: 13 minutes | **Servings**: 2

Ingredients:

- 2 store-bought flatbreads (Naan or pita bread work well)
- 1 boneless, skinless chicken breast, cooked and shredded
- 1/4 cup your favorite BBQ sauce
- 1/2 cup shredded cheddar cheese
- 1/4 cup red onion, thinly sliced
- 2 tablespoons chopped fresh cilantro
- Optional toppings: Sliced jalapenos, avocado slices, blue cheese crumbles

Directions:

1. Preheat your air fryer to 400°F (200°C).
2. Prepare the chicken: If you haven't already, cook the chicken breast according to your preferred method (grilled, baked, etc.) and shred it into bite-sized pieces.
3. Assemble the flatbreads: Spread a thin layer of BBQ sauce on each flatbread, leaving a small border around the edge.
4. Top with flavor: Divide the shredded chicken between the flatbreads, followed by the cheddar cheese and red onion.
5. Air fry it up! Place the flatbreads in the preheated air fryer and cook for 8-10 minutes, or until the cheese is melted and bubbly, and the crust is crispy.
6. Finishing touches: Garnish with fresh cilantro and any additional toppings you desire. Serve immediately and enjoy!

Nutritional Information per Serving: Calories: 450, Fat: 20g, Saturated Fat: 8g, Carbohydrates: 35g, Sugar: 10g, Protein: 30g

Tips:

- Use leftover cooked chicken for an even faster meal.
- Get creative with your toppings! Try adding sliced bell peppers, crumbled bacon, or even pineapple chunks.
- If you prefer a spicier kick, add a few dashes of hot sauce to the BBQ sauce before spreading it on the flatbreads.
- For a vegetarian option, substitute the chicken with shredded portobello mushrooms or chickpeas.
- Serve with a side salad or your favorite dipping sauce for a complete lunch.

Air Fryer Falafel Bowls

Cooking Time: 20 minutes | **Prep Time**: 15 minutes | **Total Time**: 35 minutes | **Servings**: 2

Ingredients:

For the Falafel:
- 1 cup dried chickpeas, soaked overnight
- 1/2 onion, chopped
- 2 cloves garlic, minced
- 1/2 cup fresh cilantro, chopped
- 1/4 cup fresh parsley, chopped
- 1/4 cup chickpea flour
- 1 teaspoon ground cumin
- 1/2 teaspoon coriander powder
- 1/4 teaspoon salt
- 1/4 teaspoon black pepper

For the Bowls:
- 2 cups mixed greens
- 1/2 cup cherry tomatoes, halved
- 1/4 cup crumbled feta cheese
- 1/4 cup hummus
- 2 tablespoons tahini sauce
- Lemon wedges, to taste
- Hot sauce, optional

Instructions:

1. Make the Falafel: Drain and rinse the soaked chickpeas. Place them in a food processor with the onion, garlic, cilantro, parsley, chickpea flour, cumin, coriander, salt, and pepper. Pulse until the mixture is finely chopped but not completely smooth.
2. Shape the Falafel: Form the mixture into 1-inch balls. If the mixture is too wet, add a little more chickpea flour.
3. Air Fry the Falafel: Preheat your air fryer to 400°F (200°C). Spray the air fryer basket with cooking oil. Place the falafel balls in the basket in a single layer, making sure they don't touch. Air fry for 15-20 minutes, flipping halfway through, until golden brown and crispy.
4. Assemble the Bowls: Divide the mixed greens between two bowls. Top with cherry tomatoes, crumbled feta cheese, hummus, and tahini sauce. Add the cooked falafel and drizzle with lemon juice and hot sauce, if desired.

Nutritional Information Per Serving: Calories: 450, Fat: 15g, Carbohydrates: 40g, Protein: 20g, Fiber: 5g

Tips:
- For a smoother falafel texture, remove some of the chickpea skins before processing.
- You can bake the falafel instead of air frying, if desired. Preheat the oven to 400°F (200°C) and bake for 20-25 minutes, flipping halfway through.
- Get creative with your toppings! Other options include cucumber, olives, red onion, avocado, or grilled vegetables.
- Prepare the falafel in advance and store it in an airtight container in the refrigerator for up to 3 days.
- Make this recipe vegan by using vegan feta cheese and omitting the tahini sauce.

Stuffed Portobello Mushrooms

Prep Time: 15 minutes | **Cook Time**: 15 minutes | **Total Time**: 30 minutes | **Servings**: 2

Ingredients:

- 2 large portobello mushrooms
- 1 tablespoon olive oil
- 1/4 cup chopped onion
- 1 clove garlic, minced
- 1/2 cup chopped spinach
- 1/4 cup crumbled cooked sausage (optional)
- 1/4 cup ricotta cheese
- 1/4 cup shredded mozzarella cheese
- 1/4 cup grated Parmesan cheese
- 1/4 teaspoon dried oregano
- 1/4 teaspoon dried thyme
- Salt and pepper to taste

Instructions:

1. Preheat your air fryer to 400°F (200°C). Wash the portobello mushrooms and remove the stems. Using a spoon, gently scrape out the gills from the underside of the caps. Brush the mushroom caps with olive oil and season with salt and pepper.
2. In a small pan, heat the remaining olive oil over medium heat. Add the onion and cook until softened, about 5 minutes. Stir in the garlic and cook for another minute.
3. Add the spinach to the pan and cook until wilted. Remove from heat and stir in the cooked sausage (if using).
4. In a bowl, combine the ricotta cheese, mozzarella cheese, Parmesan cheese, oregano, and thyme. Mix in the cooked spinach mixture.
5. Stuff the portobello mushroom caps with the cheese mixture, dividing evenly between them.
6. Place the stuffed mushrooms in the air fryer basket and cook for 10-12 minutes, or until the cheese is melted and bubbly and the mushrooms are tender.
7. Serve immediately, garnished with fresh herbs if desired.

Nutritional Information per Serving: Calories: 250, Fat: 10g, Carbohydrates: 20g, Fiber: 5g, Protein: 15g, Sodium: 300mg

Tips:

- For a vegetarian option, omit the sausage and use crumbled tofu or tempeh instead.
- You can adjust the amount of cheese to your liking.
- If your mushrooms are small, you may need to reduce the cooking time slightly.
- Serve with a side salad or roasted vegetables for a complete meal.

Crispy Fish Tacos

Prep Time: 10 minutes | **Cooking Time**: 15 minutes | **Total Time**: 25 minutes | **Servings**: 4

Ingredients:

For the Fish:
- 1 pound white fish fillets (cod, mahi-mahi, tilapia), cut into 1-inch strips
- 1/2 teaspoon paprika
- 1/4 teaspoon garlic powder
- 1/4 teaspoon chili powder
- Salt and pepper to taste
- 1 tablespoon olive oil

For the Toppings:
- 4 corn tortillas, warmed
- 1/2 cup shredded cabbage
- 1/4 cup diced red onion
- 1/4 cup chopped cilantro
- 1/4 cup crumbled feta cheese
- 1 avocado, sliced
- Crema or sour cream, to taste
- Lime wedges, for serving

Optional Sauce:
- 1/4 cup mayonnaise
- 1 tablespoon sriracha
- 1 tablespoon lime juice
- 1/2 teaspoon chipotle powder

Directions:

1. Prep the Fish: In a bowl, combine paprika, garlic powder, chili powder, salt, and pepper. Toss the fish strips with olive oil and then coat them in the spice mixture.
2. Cook the Fish: Preheat your air fryer to 400°F (200°C). Arrange the fish strips in a single layer, ensuring they don't touch. Air fry for 8-10 minutes, or until cooked through and golden brown. Flip the fish halfway through cooking for even browning.
3. Make the Sauce (Optional): Combine mayonnaise, sriracha, lime juice, and chipotle powder in a small bowl. Mix well and set aside.
4. Assemble the Tacos: Warm the tortillas in a microwave or pan. Divide the cooked fish, shredded cabbage, red onion, cilantro, and feta cheese evenly among the tortillas. Top with avocado slices and desired amount of crema or sour cream. Drizzle with the optional sauce if using.
5. Serve: Garnish with lime wedges and enjoy your delicious Air Fryer Crispy Fish Tacos!

Nutritional Information per serving: Calories: 350, Fat: 12g, Saturated Fat: 2g, Cholesterol: 50mg, Sodium: 350mg, Carbohydrates: 25g, Fiber: 2g, Sugar: 3g, Protein: 25g

Tips:

- For a gluten-free version, use corn tortillas.
- You can use any type of white fish you prefer.
- Feel free to adjust the spice level of the recipe to your liking.
- Serve with your favorite salsa or guacamole for added flavor and texture.
- Leftover fish can be stored in an airtight container in the refrigerator for up to 2 days.

Caprese Stuffed Chicken

Prep Time: 10 minutes | **Cook Time**: 15 minutes | **Total Time**: 25 minutes | **Servings**: 2

Ingredients:

- 2 boneless, skinless chicken breasts (about 6 oz each)
- 1/4 cup fresh basil leaves, roughly chopped
- 2 large Roma tomatoes, thinly sliced
- 4 slices mozzarella cheese
- 1 tablespoon olive oil
- 1/2 teaspoon dried oregano
- 1/4 teaspoon garlic powder
- Salt and pepper to taste

Directions:

1. Prep the Chicken: Using a sharp knife, carefully make a pocket in each chicken breast by cutting horizontally through the thickest part, but not all the way through. Season the inside of the pockets with salt and pepper.
2. Assemble the Filling: Divide the chopped basil, tomato slices, and mozzarella cheese evenly between the two chicken pockets. Secure the openings with toothpicks to prevent the filling from spilling out.
3. Season and Air Fry: In a small bowl, combine the olive oil, oregano, garlic powder, salt, and pepper. Brush the chicken breasts with the seasoning mixture. Preheat your air fryer to 400°F (200°C). Place the chicken breasts in the air fryer basket and cook for 10 minutes.
4. Flip and Finish: Carefully flip the chicken breasts and cook for an additional 5 minutes, or until the chicken is cooked through and the cheese is melted and bubbly.
5. Rest and Serve: Remove the chicken from the air fryer and let it rest for 5 minutes before serving. Garnish with additional fresh basil leaves, if desired.

Nutritional Information per serving: Calories: 350, Fat: 15g, Carbs: 5g, Protein: 40g

Tips:

- For thicker chicken breasts, you may need to increase the cooking time by a few minutes.
- Use a meat thermometer to ensure the chicken is cooked through to an internal temperature of 165°F (74°C).
- You can substitute sun-dried tomatoes for the fresh tomatoes for a different flavor profile.
- Serve with a side of roasted vegetables, salad, or quinoa for a complete meal.

Air Fryer Sweet Potato Hash

Cooking Time: 15 minutes (fish) + 15 minutes (hash) = 30 minutes | **Prep Time:** 10 minutes | **Total Time:** 40 minutes | **Serving Size:** 4 tacos

Ingredients:

For the Sweet Potato Hash:
- 1 large sweet potato, peeled and cubed
- 1 bell pepper, chopped
- 1/2 red onion, chopped
- 1 clove garlic, minced
- 1/2 teaspoon chili powder
- 1/4 teaspoon cumin
- Salt and pepper to taste
- 1 tablespoon olive oil

For the Fish:
- 4 white fish fillets (cod, tilapia, or mahi-mahi)
- 1/2 cup flour
- 1 teaspoon paprika
- 1/4 teaspoon garlic powder
- 1/4 teaspoon onion powder
- Salt and pepper to taste
- 1 egg, beaten
- 1/4 cup breadcrumbs

For the Toppings:
- 4 corn tortillas, warmed
- Avocado, sliced
- Cilantro, chopped
- Lime wedges
- Hot sauce (optional)

Instructions:

1. Prepare the Sweet Potato Hash: Preheat your air fryer to 400°F (200°C). In a large bowl, toss the sweet potato cubes, bell pepper, red onion, garlic, chili powder, cumin, salt, and pepper with olive oil.
2. Cook the Sweet Potato Hash: Spread the hash mixture in a single layer in the air fryer basket and cook for 15 minutes, shaking the basket halfway through.
3. Prepare the Fish: In a shallow dish, combine the flour, paprika, garlic powder, onion powder, salt, and pepper. In another shallow dish, whisk the egg. In a third shallow dish, place the breadcrumbs.
4. Dredge the Fish: Dredge each fish fillet in the flour mixture, then dip it in the egg, and finally coat it in the breadcrumbs.
5. Cook the Fish: Preheat your air fryer to 400°F (200°C) again if needed. Lightly spray the air fryer basket with cooking oil. Arrange the fish fillets in a single layer and cook for 7-8 minutes, or until the fish is cooked through and flaky.
6. Assemble the Tacos: Warm the tortillas in a pan or microwave. Top each tortilla with some sweet potato hash, a cooked fish fillet, avocado slices, cilantro, a squeeze of lime juice, and hot sauce (if desired).

Nutritional Information per taco: Calories: 450, Fat: 18g, Carbohydrates: 40g, Fiber: 5g, Protein: 30g

Tips:

- You can use other vegetables in the hash, such as zucchini, corn, or black beans.
- If you don't have an air fryer, you can bake the sweet potato hash in a preheated oven at 400°F (200°C) for 20-25 minutes, or pan-fry it in a skillet with a little oil.
- You can substitute any type of white fish for the cod, tilapia, or mahi-mahi.
- For a spicier taco, add some cayenne pepper to the flour mixture or the hot sauce.
- You can make these tacos ahead of time and assemble them just before serving.

Mediterranean Veggie Wraps

Cooking Time: 5 minutes per wrap | **Prep Time:** 10 minutes | **Total Time:** 15 minutes | **Serving Size:** 2 wraps

Ingredients:

- 2 whole wheat tortillas
- 1/4 cup hummus (plain or flavored)
- 1/2 cup mixed baby greens
- 1/4 cup chopped cucumber
- 1/4 cup chopped tomato
- 1/4 cup chopped red onion
- 1/4 cup crumbled feta cheese
- 1 tablespoon kalamata olives, sliced
- 1/4 teaspoon dried oregano
- Salt and pepper to taste

Directions:

1. Preheat your air fryer to 350°F (175°C).
2. Spread hummus evenly onto one half of each tortilla.
3. Top with a layer of baby greens, followed by the chopped cucumber, tomato, red onion, and feta cheese.
4. Sprinkle with oregano, olives, salt, and pepper.
5. Fold the other half of the tortilla over the filling to enclose.
6. Place the wraps in the air fryer basket, ensuring they don't touch each other.
7. Cook for 5 minutes, or until the tortillas are lightly golden and crispy.
8. Cut the wraps in half and serve immediately.

Nutritional Information per wrap: Calories: 350, Fat: 7g, Carbs: 35g, Protein: 10g

Tips:

- You can add other vegetables to your liking, such as bell peppers, zucchini, or carrots.
- If you prefer a warm filling, you can briefly saute the vegetables before adding them to the wraps.
- Use a variety of flavored hummus for different flavor profiles.
- Serve the wraps with a side of tzatziki sauce for dipping.
- If you don't have an air fryer, you can cook the wraps in a skillet over medium heat for a few minutes per side.

Crispy Coconut Shrimp

Prep Time: 10 minutes | **Cooking Time**: 8 minutes | **Total Time**: 18 minutes | **Servings**: 2

Ingredients:

- 12 large shrimp, peeled and deveined (tails on or off, optional)
- 1/4 cup all-purpose flour
- 1/2 cup unsweetened shredded coconut, lightly toasted
- 1/4 cup panko breadcrumbs
- 1 egg, beaten
- 1 tablespoon olive oil
- Salt and pepper to taste
- Sweet chili sauce, for dipping (optional)

Directions:

1. Prep the shrimp: Pat the shrimp dry with paper towels. Season them lightly with salt and pepper.
2. Set up the coating stations: In three separate shallow bowls, place the flour, beaten egg, and a mixture of the coconut and panko breadcrumbs.
3. Coat the shrimp: Dredge each shrimp in the flour, shaking off any excess. Dip them in the egg, letting any excess drip off. Finally, coat them generously in the coconut-breadcrumb mixture, pressing gently to adhere.
4. Air-fry: Preheat your air fryer to 400°F (200°C). Drizzle the shrimp lightly with olive oil. Arrange them in a single layer in the air fryer basket, ensuring they don't touch.
5. Cook: Air-fry for 8 minutes, flipping the shrimp halfway through, or until golden brown and cooked through. Be careful not to overcrowd the basket, as this will prevent even cooking.
6. Serve: Enjoy your crispy coconut shrimp immediately with a side of sweet chili sauce for dipping, if desired.

Nutritional Information per Serving: Calories: 350, Fat: 15g, Saturated Fat: 8g, Cholesterol: 150mg, Sodium: 300mg, Carbohydrates: 15g, Fiber: 2g, Sugars: 5g, Protein: 25g

Tips:

- For a thicker and crunchier coating, double-dip the shrimp in the egg and coconut-breadcrumb mixture.
- Use a digital thermometer to check the internal temperature of the shrimp. It should reach 165°F (74°C) for safe consumption.
- To toast the coconut, spread it on a baking sheet and bake at 350°F (175°C) for 5-7 minutes, stirring occasionally, until lightly golden.
- Serve your shrimp with a variety of dipping sauces, such as marinara sauce, mango chutney, or a creamy avocado sauce.
- Leftover shrimp can be stored in an airtight container in the refrigerator for up to

Air Fryer BLT Salad

Cooking Time: 15 minutes | **Prep Time**: 10 minutes | **Total Time**: 25 minutes | **Serving Size**: 2

Ingredients:

- 4 slices thick-cut bacon
- 2 slices hearty bread, cubed
- 1 cup romaine lettuce, chopped
- 1/2 cup cherry tomatoes, halved
- 1 tablespoon olive oil
- 2 tablespoons red wine vinegar
- 1 teaspoon Dijon mustard
- 1/2 teaspoon honey
- 1/4 teaspoon dried oregano
- Salt and pepper to taste

Directions:

1. Preheat your air fryer to 400°F (200°C).
2. Cook the bacon: Place the bacon in a single layer in the air fryer basket and cook for 8-10 minutes, or until crisp. Remove the bacon and transfer to a paper towel-lined plate to drain grease.
3. Toast the bread cubes: While the bacon cooks, add the bread cubes to the air fryer basket and cook for 3-5 minutes, or until golden brown. Remove and set aside.
4. Prepare the vinaigrette: In a small bowl, whisk together olive oil, red wine vinegar, Dijon mustard, honey, and oregano. Season with salt and pepper to taste.
5. Assemble the salad: In a large bowl, combine chopped romaine lettuce, cherry tomatoes, and toasted bread cubes.
6. Crumble the cooked bacon over the salad.
7. Drizzle the vinaigrette over the salad and toss to combine.
8. Serve immediately and enjoy!

Nutritional Information per serving: Calories: 450, Fat: 20g, Saturated Fat: 8g Carbohydrates: 30g, Fiber: 5g, Sugar: 5g, Protein: 20g,

Tips:

- For a vegetarian option, replace the bacon with crispy tofu or tempeh.
- Add other vegetables to the salad, such as cucumber, red onion, or avocado.
- Use a different type of bread, such as sourdough or rye, for the croutons.
- Experiment with different dressings, such as ranch or Caesar.
- Serve the salad with a side of whole-wheat crackers or pita bread for dipping.

Southwest Chicken Stuffed Peppers:

Cooking Time: 20 minutes | **Prep Time**: 15 minutes | **Total Time**: 35 minutes | **Serving Size**: 2-3 servings

Ingredients:

- 2 bell peppers (red, orange, or yellow), halved and seeds removed
- 1 pound boneless, skinless chicken breasts, cooked and shredded
- 1/2 cup black beans, rinsed and drained
- 1/4 cup frozen corn kernels
- 1/4 cup diced red onion
- 1 clove garlic, minced
- 1 tablespoon olive oil
- 1 teaspoon chili powder
- 1/2 teaspoon cumin
- 1/4 teaspoon smoked paprika
- Salt and pepper to taste
- 1/4 cup shredded cheddar cheese
- 2 tablespoons chopped fresh cilantro (optional)

Directions:

1. Preheat your air fryer to 400°F (200°C).
2. In a large bowl, combine cooked chicken, black beans, corn, red onion, garlic, olive oil, spices, salt, and pepper. Mix well.
3. Stuff each bell pepper half with the chicken mixture. Top with shredded cheese.
4. Place the stuffed peppers in the air fryer basket, ensuring they don't touch each other.
5. Air fry for 20 minutes, or until the peppers are tender and the cheese is melted and bubbly.
6. Garnish with fresh cilantro (optional) and serve immediately.

Nutritional Information per serving: Calories: 350, Fat: 15g, Carbs: 30g, Protein: 30g

Tips:

- For extra flavor, marinate the chicken in your favorite spices before cooking.
- If you don't have an air fryer, you can bake the stuffed peppers in a preheated oven at 400°F (200°C) for 25-30 minutes, or until the peppers are tender and the cheese is melted.
- Feel free to customize the recipe with your favorite vegetables, such as diced tomatoes, green bell peppers, or chopped zucchini.
- Leftovers can be stored in an airtight container in the refrigerator for up to 3 days.

DINNER RECIPES

Crispy Air Fryer Chicken Parmesan

Prep Time: 15 minutes | **Cook Time**: 15-20 minutes | **Total Time**: 30-35 minutes | **Serving Size**: 4 servings

Ingredients:

- 4 boneless, skinless chicken breasts, pounded thin
- 1/2 cup all-purpose flour
- 2 large eggs, beaten
- 1 cup Italian seasoned breadcrumbs
- 1/4 cup grated Parmesan cheese
- 1/4 teaspoon dried oregano
- 1/4 teaspoon garlic powder
- Salt and pepper to taste
- 1 jar (16 ounces) marinara sauce
- 1 cup shredded mozzarella cheese
- Fresh basil, for garnish (optional)

Directions:

1. Preheat your air fryer to 400°F (200°C).
2. Prepare three shallow bowls: one with flour, one with beaten eggs, and one with breadcrumbs mixed with Parmesan cheese, oregano, and garlic powder. Season each bowl with salt and pepper to taste.
3. Dredge each chicken breast in the flour, then dip it in the egg, and finally coat it in the breadcrumb mixture. Press the breading firmly to adhere.
4. Arrange the breaded chicken in a single layer in the air fryer basket, ensuring there's enough space between each piece for optimal airflow.
5. Cook for 10-12 minutes, flipping halfway through.
6. Remove the chicken from the air fryer and spoon 2 tablespoons of marinara sauce on top of each breast. Sprinkle with mozzarella cheese.
7. Return the chicken to the air fryer and cook for an additional 3-5 minutes, or until the cheese is melted and bubbly.
8. Garnish with fresh basil (optional) and serve immediately with remaining marinara sauce and your favorite sides, like pasta or salad.

Nutritional Information per serving: Calories: 400-500, Fat: 20g, Saturated Fat: 10g, Cholesterol: 80mg, Sodium: 500mg, Carbohydrates: 30g, Fiber: 2g, Sugar: 5g, Protein: 40g

Tips:

- If your air fryer is small, you may need to cook the chicken in batches.
- You can use panko breadcrumbs instead of Italian seasoned breadcrumbs.
- Feel free to adjust the amount of marinara sauce and cheese to your liking.
- For a healthier option, use a light marinara sauce and low-fat mozzarella cheese.
- You can also use chicken thighs instead of chicken breasts. Just be sure to adjust the cooking time accordingly.

Garlic Herb Air Fryer Salmon

Cooking Time: 8-10 minutes | **Prep Time**: 5 minutes | **Total Time**: 13-15 minutes | **Serving Size**: 2

Ingredients:

- 2 salmon fillets (6 oz each), skin-on or skinless
- 1 tablespoon olive oil
- 1 teaspoon dried Italian seasoning
- 1/2 teaspoon garlic powder
- 1/4 teaspoon salt
- 1/4 teaspoon black pepper
- 1 lemon, sliced (optional)
- Fresh herbs like parsley, dill, or chives (optional)

Directions:

1. Preheat: Preheat your air fryer to 400°F (200°C).
2. Season the Salmon: Pat the salmon fillets dry with paper towels. In a small bowl, combine olive oil, Italian seasoning, garlic powder, salt, and pepper. Rub the mixture evenly onto both sides of the salmon.
3. Air Fry: Lightly coat the air fryer basket with cooking spray or use a parchment paper liner. Place the salmon fillets in the basket, skin-side down if using skin-on salmon. Cook for 6-8 minutes, depending on the thickness of the fillets. For skin-on salmon, cook for an additional 2-3 minutes to crisp the skin.
4. Check for Doneness: Use a fork to gently flake the salmon. It's cooked through when it flakes easily and loses its translucent appearance. For precise measurement, cook to an internal temperature of 145°F (63°C) using a meat thermometer.
5. Serve: Plate the cooked salmon immediately. Garnish with lemon slices and fresh herbs, if desired. Enjoy with your favorite sides like roasted vegetables, rice, or quinoa.

Nutritional Information per Serving: Calories: 350, Fat: 18g, Protein: 35g, Carbs: 2g,

Tips:

- If using fresh herbs instead of dried, use about 1 tablespoon each of chopped parsley, dill, or chives.
- For an extra garlicky flavor, use minced fresh garlic instead of garlic powder.
- Marinate the salmon in the herb mixture for 15-30 minutes for deeper flavor.
- Experiment with different herbs and spices to create your own flavor combinations.
- Be careful not to overcook the salmon, as it can become dry.
- Cooking time may vary depending on the thickness of your salmon fillets and the specific model of your air fryer.

Stuffed Bell Peppers with Quinoa and Black Beans

Cooking Time: 25 minutes | **Prep Time**: 15 minutes | **Total Time**: 40 minutes | **Serving Size**: 4 people

Ingredients:

- 4 bell peppers (red, yellow, orange, or a mix)
- 1 cup uncooked quinoa, rinsed
- 1 15-oz can black beans, drained and rinsed
- 1/2 cup corn kernels, frozen or canned, drained
- 1/4 cup diced red onion
- 1 clove garlic, minced
- 1/2 cup chopped fresh cilantro
- 1 tablespoon olive oil
- 1 teaspoon ground cumin
- 1/2 teaspoon chili powder
- 1/4 teaspoon smoked paprika
- Salt and pepper to taste
- 1/2 cup shredded cheddar cheese (optional)

Directions:

1. Preheat your air fryer to 400°F (200°C).
2. Wash and dry the bell peppers. Cut off the tops and remove the seeds and membranes. Place the peppers upright in a baking dish.
3. In a medium saucepan, combine the quinoa and 2 cups water. Bring to a boil, then reduce heat, cover, and simmer for 15 minutes, or until the quinoa is cooked and fluffy. Fluff with a fork and set aside to cool slightly.
4. In a large bowl, combine the cooled quinoa, black beans, corn, red onion, garlic, cilantro, olive oil, cumin, chili powder, paprika, salt, and pepper. Mix well to combine.
5. Stuff the bell peppers with the quinoa mixture, dividing it evenly among them. Sprinkle with cheddar cheese, if desired.
6. Arrange the stuffed peppers in the air fryer basket, ensuring they don't touch each other. Air fry for 20-25 minutes, or until the peppers are tender and the filling is heated through.
7. Serve immediately, garnished with additional cilantro, if desired.

Nutritional Information per Serving: Calories: 350, Fat: 8g, Saturated Fat: 2g, Cholesterol: 0mg, Sodium: 350mg, Carbohydrates: 45g, Fiber: 7g, Protein: 15g

Tips:

- For a heartier dish, add cooked ground turkey or sausage to the filling.
- Substitute brown rice for the quinoa for a different texture.
- Get creative with the toppings! Try avocado slices, salsa, sour cream, or chopped green onions.
- Don't overcrowd the air fryer basket. Cook the peppers in batches if necessary.
- Leftovers can be stored in an airtight container in the refrigerator for up to 3 days. Reheat in the air fryer or microwave until warmed through.

Air Fryer Lemon Garlic Shrimp Skewers

Prep Time: 10 minutes | **Cook Time**: 8-10 minutes | **Total Time:** 20 minutes | **Serving Size:** 2-3 servings

Ingredients:

- 1 pound large shrimp, peeled and deveined
- 2 tablespoons olive oil
- 2 cloves garlic, minced
- 1 tablespoon lemon juice
- 1 teaspoon lemon zest
- 1/2 teaspoon dried oregano
- 1/4 teaspoon salt
- 1/4 teaspoon black pepper
- Wooden skewers, soaked in water for at least 30 minutes

Directions:

1. Preheat your air fryer to 400°F (200°C) for 5 minutes.
2. In a bowl, combine olive oil, garlic, lemon juice, lemon zest, oregano, salt, and pepper. Whisk well to create a marinade.
3. Add the shrimp to the marinade and toss to coat evenly. Marinate for 10 minutes.
4. Thread the shrimp onto the soaked wooden skewers. Make sure the shrimp are close together but not overcrowded on the skewers.
5. Place the shrimp skewers in a single layer in the preheated air fryer basket. Avoid overcrowding the basket for even cooking.
6. Cook for 8-10 minutes, flipping the skewers halfway through, until the shrimp are pink and cooked through. The internal temperature should reach 165°F (74°C).
7. Serve immediately with your favorite dipping sauce, such as lemon wedges, marinara sauce, or aioli.

Nutritional Information: Calories: 220 per serving, Fat: 10g, Carbohydrates: 2g, Protein: 25g, Sodium: 400mg (adjust according to your preference)

Tips:

- For a spicier kick, add a pinch of red pepper flakes to the marinade.
- You can substitute fresh herbs, such as parsley or dill, for the dried oregano.
- Serve the skewers over a bed of rice, quinoa, or couscous for a complete meal.
- Leftover cooked shrimp can be stored in an airtight container in the refrigerator for up to 3 days.

BBQ Pulled Pork Sliders with Coleslaw

Cooking Time: 1 hour 15 minutes | **Prep Time**: 15 minutes | **Total Time**: 1 hour 30 minutes | **Serving Size**: 6-8 servings

Ingredients:

For the Pulled Pork:
- 1 lb boneless pork shoulder, trimmed and cut into 1-inch cubes
- 1 tbsp olive oil
- 1 tsp paprika
- 1 tsp ground cumin
- 1/2 tsp onion powder
- 1/2 tsp garlic powder
- 1/4 tsp salt
- 1/4 tsp black pepper
- 1/2 cup chicken broth
- 1/4 cup your favorite BBQ sauce

For the Coleslaw:
- 1/2 head green cabbage, thinly shredded
- 1/4 head red cabbage, thinly shredded
- 1 carrot, grated
- 2 tbsp mayonnaise
- 1 tbsp apple cider vinegar
- 1 tsp Dijon mustard
- 1/2 tsp sugar
- 1/4 tsp salt
- 1/4 tsp black pepper

For the Sliders:
- 12 mini slider buns
- Optional: melted butter, paprika, and sesame seeds for topping

Instructions:

1. Marinate the pork: In a large bowl, toss the pork cubes with olive oil, paprika, cumin, onion powder, garlic powder, salt, and pepper. Cover and refrigerate for at least 30 minutes, or up to overnight.
2. Cook the pork: Preheat your air fryer to 400°F (200°C). Add the marinated pork cubes in a single layer to the air fryer basket. Cook for 20 minutes, flipping halfway through.
3. Shred the pork: Carefully remove the pork from the air fryer and shred it using two forks. Drain any excess liquid.
4. Make the sauce: In a small bowl, whisk together the chicken broth and BBQ sauce. Set aside.
5. Assemble the sliders: Place the bottom halves of the slider buns in the air fryer basket. Top with shredded pork and drizzle with the BBQ sauce mixture.
6. Bake the sliders: Cook for 5-7 minutes, or until the buns are toasted and the sauce is bubbly.
7. Make the coleslaw: In a large bowl, combine the shredded cabbage, carrot, mayonnaise, apple cider vinegar, Dijon mustard, sugar, salt, and pepper. Toss to coat evenly.
8. Assemble the final sliders: Top the cooked sliders with a spoonful of coleslaw. Add the bun tops and rush with melted butter, if desired. Sprinkle with paprika and sesame seeds for extra flavor.
9. Serve immediately and enjoy!

Nutritional Information per serving: Calories: 450, Fat: 18g, Saturated Fat: 6g, Cholesterol: 80mg, Sodium: 500mg, Carbohydrates: 40g, Fiber: 3g, Sugar: 10g, Protein: 30g

Tips:

- You can use pre-shredded pork shoulder to save time.
- For a sweeter coleslaw, add a tablespoon of honey to the dressing.
- If you don't have an air fryer, you can bake the sliders in a preheated oven at 400°F (200°C) for 10-12 minutes, or until the buns are golden brown and the sauce is bubbly.
- Get creative with your toppings! Add pickles, red onion, jalapeños, or your favorite cheese to the sliders.

Crispy Air Fryer Tofu Stir-Fry

Cooking Time: 20 minutes | **Prep Time**: 10 minutes | **Total Time**: 30 minutes | **Servings**: 2

Ingredients:

For the Tofu:
- 1 block (14 oz) extra-firm tofu, pressed and drained
- 1 tablespoon soy sauce
- 1 tablespoon cornstarch
- 1/2 teaspoon garlic powder
- 1/4 teaspoon black pepper

For the Stir-Fry:

- 1 tablespoon avocado oil
- 1 bell pepper, sliced
- 1/2 onion, sliced
- 1 cup broccoli florets
- 1/2 cup snap peas
- 1/4 cup chopped carrots
- 1/4 cup stir-fry sauce (your favorite)
- Sesame seeds, for garnish (optional)

Directions:

1. Prepare the Tofu:
2. Cut the tofu into bite-sized cubes.
3. In a bowl, combine the soy sauce, cornstarch, garlic powder, and black pepper. Add the tofu and toss to coat evenly.
4. Air Fry the Tofu:
5. Preheat your air fryer to 400°F (200°C).
6. Arrange the tofu cubes in a single layer in the air fryer basket. Avoid overcrowding, cook in batches if necessary.
7. Air fry for 10-12 minutes, flipping halfway through, or until golden brown and crispy.
8. Cook the Vegetables:
9. While the tofu is cooking, heat the avocado oil in a large skillet or wok over medium heat.
10. Add the bell pepper, onion, and broccoli florets and stir-fry for 3-4 minutes, until slightly softened.
11. Add the snap peas and carrots and stir-fry for another 2-3 minutes, until crisp-tender.
12. Assemble the Stir-Fry:
13. Add the cooked tofu and stir-fry sauce to the vegetables. Toss to coat everything evenly.
14. Heat through for another minute or two, until the sauce is warmed and bubbly.
15. Serve and Enjoy:
16. Transfer the stir-fry to plates and garnish with sesame seeds, if desired.
17. Serve immediately with rice or noodles.

Nutritional Information per Serving: Calories: 350, Fat: 15g, Carbohydrates: 25g, Protein: 20g

Tips:

- To press the tofu more efficiently, wrap it in a clean kitchen towel and place a heavy object on top for at least 15 minutes.
- For extra crispy tofu, use a cornstarch and breadcrumbs coating instead of just cornstarch.
- Customize the stir-fry with your favorite vegetables and sauce. Some popular options include broccoli, mushrooms, zucchini, teriyaki sauce, peanut sauce, or sweet and sour sauce.
- Serve this stir-fry with brown rice, quinoa, or noodles for a complete and satisfying meal.

Buffalo Chicken Stuffed Sweet Potatoes

Cooking Time: 20 minutes | **Prep Time**: 10 minutes | **Total Time**: 30 minutes | **Servings**: 2

Ingredients:

- 2 medium sweet potatoes
- 1 tablespoon olive oil
- 1/2 teaspoon paprika
- 1/4 teaspoon garlic powder
- 1/4 teaspoon onion powder
- 1/4 teaspoon salt
- 1 pound boneless, skinless chicken breasts, cooked and shredded
- 1/2 cup buffalo sauce (adjust for desired heat level)
- 1 tablespoon melted butter or ghee (optional)
- 1/4 cup crumbled blue cheese
- Chopped green onions, for garnish
- Ranch dressing, for drizzling (optional)

Instructions:

1. **Preheat**: Preheat your air fryer to 400°F (200°C).
2. **Prepare the sweet potatoes**: Wash and scrub the sweet potatoes. Pierce each potato with a fork several times. Rub with olive oil and sprinkle with paprika, garlic powder, onion powder, and salt.
3. **Air-fry the sweet potatoes**: Place the sweet potatoes in the air fryer basket and cook for 20 minutes, flipping halfway through, or until tender when pierced with a fork.
4. **Meanwhile, cook the chicken**: If you haven't already, cook the chicken breasts according to your preferred method (poaching, baking, grilling, etc.). Shred the cooked chicken into bite-sized pieces.
5. **Make the buffalo sauce**: In a bowl, combine the buffalo sauce and melted butter (if using). Toss the shredded chicken in the buffalo sauce mixture until evenly coated.
6. **Assemble**: Once the sweet potatoes are cooked, carefully cut them open lengthwise, leaving a hinge on one side. Fluff the flesh slightly with a fork.
7. **Stuff and top**: Divide the buffalo chicken mixture between the sweet potato halves. Top with blue cheese crumbles and green onions.
8. **Serve**: Drizzle with ranch dressing, if desired, and serve immediately. Enjoy!

Nutritional Information per Serving: Calories: 450, Fat: 15g, Carbohydrates: 40g, Protein: 30g, Sodium: 400mg

Tips:

- For a crispier sweet potato skin, brush with additional olive oil before air-frying.
- To add vegetables, stir chopped broccoli, bell peppers, or onions into the buffalo chicken mixture.
- Leftover cooked chicken or rotisserie chicken can be used for convenience.
- Adjust the amount of hot sauce to your desired level of spiciness.
- For a dairy-free option, omit the blue cheese and ranch dressing.
- Serve with additional air-fried vegetables or a side salad for a complete meal.

Crispy Breaded Air Fryer Pork Chops

Prep Time: 10 minutes | **Cooking Time**: 12 minutes | **Total Time**: 22 minutes | **Servings**: 2

Ingredients:

- 2 boneless, center-cut pork chops (about 6-8 ounces each)
- 1/4 teaspoon salt
- 1/4 teaspoon black pepper
- 1/4 cup all-purpose flour
- 1 large egg, beaten
- 1/2 cup panko breadcrumbs
- 1/4 cup grated Parmesan cheese
- 1 tablespoon Italian seasoning
- 1/2 teaspoon garlic powder
- 1/4 teaspoon onion powder
- Cooking spray

Instructions:

1. Prep the Pork Chops: Pat the pork chops dry with paper towels. Season both sides with salt and pepper.
2. Set Up the Breading Station: Prepare three shallow bowls. In the first bowl, place the flour. In the second bowl, whisk the egg. In the third bowl, combine the panko breadcrumbs, Parmesan cheese, Italian seasoning, garlic powder, and onion powder.
3. Bread the Pork Chops: Dredge each pork chop in the flour, shaking off any excess. Dip the coated chop in the egg wash, letting the excess drip off. Finally, coat the pork chop generously in the breadcrumb mixture, pressing to adhere.
4. Preheat the Air Fryer: Preheat your air fryer to 400°F (200°C).
5. Cook the Pork Chops: Lightly spray the air fryer basket with cooking spray. Arrange the breaded pork chops in a single layer, making sure they are not touching. Cook for 6 minutes, then flip the chops and cook for an additional 6 minutes, or until the internal temperature of the pork chops reaches 145°F (63°C) as measured by a meat thermometer.
6. Serve: Enjoy your crispy breaded air fryer pork chops immediately with your favorite sides.

Nutritional Information per serving: Calories: 350, Fat: 18g, Saturated Fat: 6g, Cholesterol: 80mg, Sodium: 450mg, Carbohydrates: 10g, Fiber: 1g, Sugar: 2g, Protein: 35g

Tips:

- For thicker pork chops, increase the cooking time by 2-3 minutes per side.
- You can substitute other seasonings for the Italian seasoning, such as Cajun seasoning, paprika, or your own favorite blend.
- For a gluten-free option, use gluten-free flour and breadcrumbs.
- Serve with a dipping sauce, such as Dijon mustard, honey mustard, or barbecue sauce.

Vegetarian Eggplant Parmesan

Cook Time: 20-25 minutes | **Prep Time:** 15 minutes | **Total Time:** 35-40 minutes | **Serving Size:** 4 servings

Ingredients:

- 1 medium eggplant, sliced into 1/2-inch rounds
- Salt and pepper to taste
- 1/4 cup flour
- 1/2 cup panko breadcrumbs
- 1 tablespoon olive oil
- 1 jar (24 oz) marinara sauce
- 1 cup shredded mozzarella cheese
- 1/4 cup grated Parmesan cheese (optional)
- Fresh basil leaves, for garnish (optional)

Directions:

1. Prepare the eggplant: Preheat your air fryer to 400°F (200°C). Lightly sprinkle both sides of the eggplant slices with salt and pepper. Let them sit for 10 minutes, then pat them dry with paper towels.
2. Bread the eggplant: Set up three shallow bowls: one with flour, one with beaten eggs (optional), and one with panko breadcrumbs mixed with Italian seasoning (optional). Dip each eggplant slice in flour, then the egg (if using), and finally, coat it evenly with the panko mixture.
3. Air fry the eggplant: Spray the air fryer basket with cooking spray. Arrange the breaded eggplant slices in a single layer, ensuring they don't touch. Air fry for 5-7 minutes per side, or until golden brown and crispy. Flip halfway through cooking.
4. Assemble the casserole: Spread a thin layer of marinara sauce in the bottom of a baking dish or air fryer-safe casserole dish. Arrange half of the cooked eggplant slices over the sauce. Top with half of the mozzarella cheese and a sprinkle of Parmesan cheese (if using). Repeat with the remaining eggplant, sauce, and cheese.
5. Bake: Bake the casserole in a preheated oven at 400°F (200°C) for 10-15 minutes, or until the cheese is melted and bubbly. Alternatively, if your air fryer has a baking function, use it at 400°F (200°C) for 5-7 minutes.
6. Serve: Garnish with fresh basil leaves (optional) and serve immediately.

Nutritional Information per serving: Calories: 350, Fat: 15g, Saturated Fat: 6g, Cholesterol: 10mg, Sodium: 400mg, Carbohydrates: 30g, Fiber: 4g, Sugar: 10g, Protein: 15g

Tips:

- To remove bitterness from the eggplant, sprinkle the slices with salt and let them sit for 30 minutes before rinsing and patting them dry.
- You can use a gluten-free flour blend and gluten-free breadcrumbs for a gluten-free version.
- For a vegan option, use vegan marinara sauce and vegan cheese shreds.
- Add other vegetables to the marinara sauce, such as chopped mushrooms, peppers, or onions.
- Leftovers can be stored in an airtight container in the refrigerator for up to 3 days. Reheat in the air fryer or oven until warmed through.

Honey Garlic Air Fryer Chicken Thighs

Prep Time: 15 minutes | **Cook Time**: 20-25 minutes | **Total Time**: 35-40 minutes | **Servings**: 4

Ingredients:

- 4 boneless, skinless chicken thighs
- 1/4 cup soy sauce
- 2 tablespoons honey
- 2 tablespoons rice vinegar
- 1 tablespoon olive oil
- 2 cloves garlic, minced
- 1 teaspoon grated ginger (optional)
- 1/2 teaspoon black pepper
- 1/4 teaspoon sriracha (optional)
- Salt, to taste
- Sesame seeds, for garnish (optional)

Directions:

1. Marinate the chicken: In a bowl, whisk together soy sauce, honey, rice vinegar, olive oil, garlic, ginger (if using), black pepper, and sriracha (if using). Add the chicken thighs and toss to coat completely. Cover the bowl and refrigerate for at least 30 minutes, or up to overnight for deeper flavor.
2. Preheat the air fryer: Preheat your air fryer to 400°F (200°C) for 5 minutes.
3. Air fry the chicken: Remove the chicken thighs from the marinade, letting any excess drip off. Arrange the chicken thighs in a single layer in the air fryer basket, ensuring they don't touch.
4. Cook and flip: Air fry for 12-15 minutes, then flip the chicken thighs and cook for another 8-10 minutes, or until the internal temperature reaches 165°F (74°C) using a meat thermometer inserted into the thickest part of the thigh.
5. Broil for crispier skin (optional): If desired, switch your air fryer to the broil setting for the last 2-3 minutes of cooking for extra crispy skin. Watch closely to avoid burning.
6. Rest and serve: Transfer the chicken thighs to a plate and let them rest for 5 minutes before serving. Garnish with sesame seeds (optional) and enjoy with your favorite sides.

Nutritional Information per serving: Calories: 350-400, Fat: 20-25g, Protein: 35-40g, Carbs: 10-15g

Tips:

- You can use bone-in, skin-on chicken thighs for a richer flavor, but increase the cooking time by 5-10 minutes.
- Use a combination of cornstarch and paprika for a crispy coating before air frying.
- Drizzle the chicken with the remaining marinade during the last few minutes of cooking for additional flavor.
- Serve with roasted vegetables, rice, or mashed potatoes for a complete meal.

Cajun Shrimp and Sausage Foil Packets

Cooking Time: 15 minutes | **Prep Time**: 10 minutes | **Total Time**: 25 minutes | **Serving Size:** 2 Packets (easily customizable for more servings)

Ingredients:

- 1 pound large shrimp, peeled and deveined
- 8 ounces smoked sausage, sliced
- 1 bell pepper, chopped
- 1/2 onion, chopped
- 1 clove garlic, minced
-
- 1 tablespoon olive oil
- 2 tablespoons Cajun seasoning
- 1/4 cup chopped fresh parsley, for garnish (optional)
- Lemon wedges, for serving (optional)

Directions:

1. Prep the filling: In a large bowl, combine shrimp, sausage, bell pepper, onion, garlic, olive oil, and Cajun seasoning. Toss well to coat all ingredients evenly.
2. Assemble the packets: Cut two large sheets of aluminum foil into squares. Divide the shrimp and sausage mixture evenly between the two foil squares.
3. Fold and seal: Fold the opposite sides of each foil square over the filling, then fold the ends up tightly to create sealed packets. Ensure the packets are secure to prevent leaks.
4. Air fry: Preheat your air fryer to 400°F (200°C). Place the foil packets in the air fryer basket, ensuring they don't touch each other.
5. Cook: Cook for 15 minutes, or until the shrimp are pink and opaque and the sausage is cooked through. You can check for doneness by carefully opening a packet slightly and peeking inside.
6. Rest and serve: Let the packets cool for a few minutes before carefully opening them on plates. Garnish with fresh parsley and serve with lemon wedges, if desired.

Nutritional Information approximate per serving: Calories: 400, Fat: 15g, Protein: 30g, Carbs: 15g, Sodium: 500mg

Tips:

- For a spicier kick, add a pinch of cayenne pepper to the Cajun seasoning.
- You can substitute other vegetables like zucchini, corn, or asparagus for the bell pepper and onion.
- If your air fryer has a smaller capacity, cook the packets in batches to ensure even cooking.
- Feel free to adjust the amount of Cajun seasoning to your taste preference.
- Serve with cooked rice, quinoa, or crusty bread for a complete meal.

Beef and Vegetable Kabobs with Chimichurri Sauce

Cooking Time: 15 minutes | **Prep Time**: 10 minutes | **Total Time**: 25 minutes | **Serving Size**: 4

Ingredients:

For the Beef and Vegetables:
- 1 pound flank steak, trimmed and cut into 1-inch cubes
- 1 bell pepper, cut into 1-inch chunks
- 1 red onion, cut into 1-inch wedges
- 1 zucchini, cut into 1-inch chunks
- 1 tablespoon olive oil
- 1/2 teaspoon salt
- 1/4 teaspoon black pepper
- 16 wooden skewers, soaked in water for 30 minutes

For the Chimichurri Sauce:
- 1/2 cup fresh parsley, chopped
- 1/4 cup fresh cilantro, chopped
- 1 clove garlic, minced
- 1/4 cup red onion, finely chopped
- 2 tablespoons red wine vinegar
- 1/4 cup extra virgin olive oil
- 1/4 teaspoon red pepper flakes (optional)
- 1/2 teaspoon salt
- 1/4 teaspoon black pepper

Instructions:

1. Prepare the Chimichurri Sauce: Combine all chimichurri ingredients in a food processor or blender and pulse until finely chopped but still slightly chunky. Set aside.
2. Marinate the Beef: In a bowl, toss the beef cubes with olive oil, salt, and pepper. Marinate for at least 10 minutes, or up to 30 minutes for more flavor.
3. Assemble the Skewers: Thread beef cubes, bell pepper pieces, red onion wedges, and zucchini chunks onto the soaked skewers, alternating ingredients for even cooking.
4. Air Fry the Kabobs: Preheat your air fryer to 400°F (200°C). Arrange the skewers in a single layer in the air fryer basket, ensuring they don't touch. Air fry for 10-12 minutes, flipping halfway through, or until the beef reaches desired doneness (160°F for medium).
5. Rest and Serve: Let the kabobs rest for a few minutes before serving. Drizzle generously with chimichurri sauce and enjoy!

Nutritional Information per Serving: Calories: 350, Fat: 15g, Protein: 30g, Carbohydrates: 10g

Tips:

- Use other vegetables like cherry tomatoes, mushrooms, or pineapple chunks for variety.
- For a thicker chimichurri sauce, reduce the amount of red wine vinegar or pulse less in the food processor.
- Marinate the beef overnight for even deeper flavor.
- Serve the kabobs with additional chimichurri sauce on the side for dipping.
- Substitute chicken breasts or thighs for the beef, adjusting cooking time accordingly.

Southwest Stuffed Peppers with Ground Turkey

Cooking Time: 25 minutes | **Prep Time**: 15 minutes | **Total Time**: 40 minutes | **Servings**: 4

Ingredients:

- 4 bell peppers (any color), halved and seeded
- 1 tablespoon olive oil
- 1/2 onion, diced
- 1 clove garlic, minced
- 1 pound ground turkey (93% lean)
- 1/2 teaspoon chili powder
- 1/2 teaspoon cumin
- 1/4 teaspoon smoked paprika
- 1/4 teaspoon cayenne pepper (optional, for added heat)
- 1 (15 oz) can black beans, drained and rinsed
- 1 (15 oz) can corn, drained
- 1/2 cup diced tomatoes
- 1/4 cup chopped fresh cilantro
- 1/2 cup shredded Monterey Jack cheese
- Salt and pepper to taste

Directions:

1. Preheat your air fryer to 400°F (200°C).
2. Prepare the peppers: Cut the bell peppers in half lengthwise and remove the seeds and membranes. Rinse and pat dry.
3. Saute the filling: Heat olive oil in a large skillet over medium heat. Add the onion and cook until softened, about 5 minutes. Add the garlic and cook for another minute until fragrant.
4. Brown the ground turkey: Add the ground turkey to the skillet and break it up with a spoon as it cooks. Season with chili powder, cumin, paprika, and cayenne pepper (if using). Cook until the turkey is browned and cooked through, about 7-8 minutes.
5. Assemble the filling: Drain any excess fat from the pan. Add the black beans, corn, tomatoes, and cilantro to the cooked turkey mixture. Stir to combine and season with salt and pepper to taste.
6. Stuff the peppers: Divide the filling evenly among the prepared bell pepper halves. Top each pepper with shredded Monterey Jack cheese.
7. Air fry the peppers: Arrange the stuffed peppers upright in your air fryer basket. If your air fryer doesn't have enough space for all the peppers at once, cook them in batches.
8. Cook for 20-25 minutes, or until the peppers are tender and the cheese is melted and bubbly.
9. Serve immediately! Garnish with additional cilantro, sour cream, salsa, or your favorite toppings, if desired.

Nutritional Information per serving: Calories: 400, Fat: 15g, Saturated Fat: 5g, Protein: 30g, Carbohydrates: 30g, Fiber: 5g, Sodium: 400mg

Tips:

- For a vegetarian option, replace the ground turkey with crumbled tofu or lentils.
- You can use different colored bell peppers for a more colorful dish.
- Adjust the amount of spice to your liking.
- Serve these peppers with a side of brown rice, quinoa, or salad for a complete meal.

Crispy Coconut Shrimp with Mango Salsa

Cooking Time: 10 minutes | **Prep Time**: 15 minutes | **Total Time**: 25 minutes | Serving Size: 4

Ingredients:

For the Shrimp:
- 1 pound large shrimp, peeled and deveined
- 1/2 cup all-purpose flour
- 1/4 cup cornstarch
- 1/2 teaspoon paprika
- 1/4 teaspoon garlic powder
- 1/4 teaspoon onion powder
- 1/4 teaspoon salt
- 1/4 teaspoon black pepper
- 1 large egg, beaten
- 1/2 cup unsweetened shredded coconut
- Cooking spray

For the Mango Salsa:
- 1 ripe mango, peeled and diced
- 1/2 red onion, finely diced
- 1/4 cup chopped cilantro
- 1 tablespoon lime juice
- 1 teaspoon honey
- 1/4 teaspoon chili flakes (optional)
- Salt and pepper to taste

Directions:

1. Prepare the Mango Salsa: In a medium bowl, combine mango, red onion, cilantro, lime juice, honey, chili flakes (if using), salt, and pepper. Stir well and set aside.
2. Prepare the Shrimp: In a shallow bowl, whisk together flour, cornstarch, paprika, garlic powder, onion powder, salt, and pepper. In another shallow bowl, whisk the egg. Spread the shredded coconut on a plate.
3. Dredge each shrimp in the flour mixture, then dip in the egg, and finally coat in the shredded coconut. Ensure the shrimp are evenly coated.
4. Preheat your air fryer to 400°F (200°C). Arrange the shrimp in a single layer in the air fryer basket, making sure they don't touch. Lightly spray the shrimp with cooking spray.
5. Air fry for 8-10 minutes, or until the shrimp are golden brown and cooked through. Flip the shrimp halfway through cooking for even browning.
6. Serve the shrimp hot with the mango salsa for dipping.

Tips:

- For a spicier kick, add a pinch of cayenne pepper to the flour mixture.
- You can use panko breadcrumbs instead of shredded coconut for a different texture.
- Serve the shrimp with a side of steamed rice or quinoa for a complete meal.
- For leftovers, store the shrimp in an airtight container in the refrigerator for up to 2 days. Reheat in the air fryer at 350°F (175°C) for a few minutes until crispy.

Teriyaki Salmon with Stir-Fried Vegetables

Cooking Time: 15 minutes | **Prep Time:** 10 minutes | **Total Time:** 25-27 minutes | **Serving Size:** 2

Ingredients:

- For the Teriyaki Salmon:
- 2 (6 oz) skinless salmon fillets
- 1/4 cup low-sodium teriyaki sauce
- 1 tablespoon soy sauce
- 1 teaspoon brown sugar
- 1 teaspoon grated ginger
- 1 clove garlic, minced
- 1/2 teaspoon sesame oil

For the Stir-Fried Vegetables:
- 1 tablespoon vegetable oil
- 1 cup mixed stir-fry vegetables (such as broccoli florets, bell peppers, snap peas, carrots)
- 1/4 cup frozen peas
- 1/4 cup water or low-sodium chicken broth
- 1 tablespoon soy sauce
- 1/2 teaspoon cornstarch
- Salt and pepper to taste
- Sesame seeds, for garnish (optional)

Directions:

1. Marinate the Salmon: In a small bowl, whisk together teriyaki sauce, soy sauce, brown sugar, ginger, garlic, and sesame oil. Place salmon fillets in a shallow dish and pour the marinade over, coating both sides. Let marinate for at least 10 minutes, or up to 30 minutes for deeper flavor.
2. Preheat Air Fryer: Preheat your air fryer to 400°F (200°C).
3. Cook the Salmon: Arrange the salmon fillets in a single layer in the air fryer basket. Air fry for 12-15 minutes, or until cooked through and flaky. The internal temperature should reach 145°F (63°C).
4. While the salmon cooks, prepare the vegetables: In a large bowl, combine stir-fry vegetables and frozen peas. Toss to coat
5. Stir-fry the vegetables: In a large skillet or wok, heat vegetable oil over medium-high heat. Add the vegetables and stir-fry for 3-4 minutes, until slightly softened.
6. Make the sauce: In a small bowl, whisk together water or broth, soy sauce, and cornstarch. Pour the sauce into the pan with the vegetables and cook for 1-2 minutes, or until thickened and slightly bubbly.
7. Serve: Divide the stir-fried vegetables between two plates. Top each plate with a cooked salmon fillet. Drizzle with any remaining teriyaki sauce from the air fryer basket, if desired. Garnish with sesame seeds, if using.

Nutritional Information Per Serving: Calories: 450, Fat: 20g, Protein: 35g, Carbs: 20g

Tips:

- Use a meat thermometer to ensure the salmon is cooked through to an internal temperature of 145°F (63°C).
- For a crispier salmon, preheat the air fryer for 5 minutes before adding the salmon.
- Feel free to adjust the vegetables to your preference. Other options include snow peas, baby corn, or green beans.

- Serve with rice or quinoa for a complete meal.

FAST FOOD FOR GOOD HEALTH

Air-Fried Sweet Potato Fries

Prep Time: 10 minutes | **Cook Time**: 15-20 minutes | **Total Time**: 25-30 minutes | **Serving Size**: 2-3 people

Ingredients:

- 2 medium sweet potatoes
- 1 tablespoon olive oil
- 1/2 teaspoon dried thyme
- 1/2 teaspoon garlic powder
- 1/4 teaspoon smoked paprika
- 1/4 teaspoon cayenne pepper (optional)
- Salt and freshly ground black pepper, to taste

Directions:

1. Preheat your air fryer to 400°F (200°C).
2. Wash and scrub the sweet potatoes.
3. Decide if you want to peel them: Peeling is optional, but it will result in crispier fries. If you don't peel, make sure to scrub them well to remove any dirt.
4. Cut the sweet potatoes into evenly sized sticks. Aim for thickness of around 1/4 inch for fries, or 1/2 inch for wedges.
5. In a large bowl, toss the sweet potato sticks with olive oil. Make sure they are all evenly coated.
6. Add the thyme, garlic powder, paprika, and cayenne pepper (if using) to the bowl. Season generously with salt and black pepper. Toss again to coat evenly.
7. Arrange the sweet potato sticks in a single layer in the air fryer basket. Do not overcrowd the basket, as this will prevent them from crisping properly. You may need to cook in batches depending on the size of your air fryer.
8. Air fry for 15-20 minutes, or until the fries are golden brown and crispy. Shake the basket halfway through cooking to ensure even browning.
9. Serve immediately with your favorite dipping sauce. Enjoy!

Nutritional Information per Serving : Calories: 200, Fat: 5g, Carbohydrates: 30g, Fiber: 3g, Sugar: 5g, Protein: 2g

Tips:

- For extra crispy fries, soak the sweet potato sticks in cold water for 30 minutes before drying them thoroughly and proceeding with the recipe.
- Experiment with different spices and herbs to find your favorite flavor combination. Some other options include cumin, cinnamon, chili powder, or Italian seasoning.

- If you don't have an air fryer, you can also bake these fries in a preheated oven at 425°F (220°C) for 20-25 minutes, flipping them halfway through cooking.

Air-Fried Chicken Tenders

Prep Time: 10 minute | **Cook Time**: 10-12 minutes | **Total Time**: 20-22 minutes | **Serving Size**: 4 tenders

Ingredients:

- 1 pound boneless, skinless chicken tenders
- 1/4 cup all-purpose flour
- 1 large egg, beaten
- 1/2 cup panko breadcrumbs
- 1 teaspoon paprika
- 1/2 teaspoon garlic powder
- 1/4 teaspoon onion powder
- 1/4 teaspoon salt
- 1/4 teaspoon black pepper
- Cooking spray

Directions:

1. Prepare the chicken: Cut the chicken tenders into equal-sized strips, about 1-inch thick. Pat them dry with paper towels.
2. Set up the breading station: Place the flour in one shallow bowl, the beaten egg in another, and the breadcrumb mixture (combine panko, paprika, garlic powder, onion powder, salt, and pepper) in a third bowl.
3. Breading: Dredge each chicken tender in the flour, then the egg, and finally the breadcrumb mixture, ensuring good coverage. Shake off any excess.
4. Preheat the air fryer: Preheat your air fryer to 400°F (200°C).
5. Air fry the chicken: Lightly spray the air fryer basket with cooking spray. Arrange the chicken tenders in a single layer, ensuring they don't touch. Air fry for 8-10 minutes, flipping halfway through cooking.
6. Cook until done: Continue cooking until the chicken tenders are golden brown and cooked through, reaching an internal temperature of 165°F (74°C) as measured by a food thermometer.
7. Serve and enjoy: Serve your Air-Fried Chicken Tenders hot with your favorite dipping sauces like honey mustard, BBQ sauce, or ranch dressing.

Nutritional Information: Calories: 300 per serving, Fat: 15g, Saturated Fat: 5g, Protein: 30g Carbohydrates: 5g, Fiber: 1g

Tips:

You can use various breadcrumb alternatives like crushed oats, crushed almond flour, or whole-wheat breadcrumbs for a healthier twist.
For extra crispy tenders, double dip them in the egg and breadcrumb mixture.
Don't overcrowd the air fryer basket, as this will prevent even cooking. Cook in batches if necessary.

Cooking times may vary slightly depending on the thickness of your chicken tenders and your air fryer model.

Air-Fried Buffalo Cauliflower Wings

Prep Time: 15 minutes | **Cook Time**: 12-15 minutes | **Total Time**: 27-30 minutes | **Servings**: 4

Ingredients:

- 1 head cauliflower, cut into florets
- 1 tablespoon olive oil or avocado oil
- 1/2 teaspoon garlic powder
- 1/2 teaspoon smoked paprika
- 1/4 teaspoon onion powder
- Salt and pepper to taste
- 1/2 cup your favorite buffalo sauce (choose a low-sugar option for "Fast food for good health")
- Optional toppings: blue cheese crumbles, chopped celery, carrot sticks

Instructions:

1. Preheat your air fryer to 400°F (200°C).
2. In a large bowl, toss the cauliflower florets with the olive oil, garlic powder, paprika, onion powder, salt, and pepper. Ensure all florets are evenly coated.
3. Arrange the cauliflower florets in a single layer in the air fryer basket, avoiding overcrowding.
4. Air fry for 12-15 minutes, flipping halfway through, until the cauliflower is tender and slightly browned.
5. In a separate bowl, toss the cooked cauliflower with the buffalo sauce. Coat to your desired level of spiciness.
6. Air fry for an additional 2-3 minutes to heat the sauce and crisp up the cauliflower further.
7. Serve immediately with your desired toppings, such as blue cheese crumbles, chopped celery, and carrot sticks.

Nutritional Information per serving, estimated: Calories: 200-250 .Fat: 6-8g, Saturated Fat: 2-3g, Cholesterol: 0mg, Sodium: 300-400mg, Carbohydrates: 20-25g, Fiber: 3-4g, Sugar: 5-7g, Protein: 5-7g

Tips:

- For a thicker coating, try adding 1/4 cup chickpea flour or whole wheat flour to the dry ingredients before tossing with the cauliflower.
- You can adjust the cooking time depending on the size of your cauliflower florets and the desired level of crispness.
- For a vegan option, choose a vegan buffalo sauce and omit the blue cheese crumbles.
- You can also use pre-cut cauliflower florets to save time on prep.
- To add a smoky flavor, sprinkle the cauliflower with smoked paprika before air frying.

- Experiment with different dipping sauces, such as ranch dressing or vegan blue cheese dip.

Air-Fried Turkey Burgers:

Prep Time: 10 minutes | **Cook Time:** 12-15 minutes | **Total Time**: 22-27 minute | **Servings**: 4

Ingredients:

- 1 pound lean ground turkey (90% lean or higher)
- 1/4 cup finely chopped onion
- 1/4 cup chopped fresh parsley
- 2 tablespoons low-fat mayonnaise
- 1 tablespoon Worcestershire sauce
- 1 teaspoon dried oregano
- 1/2 teaspoon garlic powder
- 1/2 teaspoon onion powder
- 1/4 teaspoon black pepper
- 1/4 teaspoon salt (optional)
- 4 whole-wheat hamburger buns, toasted (optional)
- Lettuce, tomato, onion, and your favorite burger toppings

Instructions:

1. In a large bowl, combine the ground turkey, onion, parsley, mayonnaise, Worcestershire sauce, oregano, garlic powder, onion powder, pepper, and salt (if using). Mix gently until just combined. Don't overmix, as this can make the burgers tough.
2. Divide the mixture into 4 equal portions and form them into patties. Make a slight indentation in the center of each patty to prevent them from puffing up too much while cooking.
3. Preheat your air fryer to 400°F (200°C). Lightly spray the air fryer basket with cooking spray.
4. Arrange the burgers in the air fryer basket in a single layer, ensuring they don't touch.
5. Air fry for 12-15 minutes, flipping the burgers halfway through, until cooked through and reaching an internal temperature of 165°F (74°C).
6. Meanwhile, toast the hamburger buns (if using).
7. Assemble the burgers with your desired toppings on the toasted buns (if using).

Nutritional Information per serving: Calories: 250, Fat: 9g, Saturated Fat: 3g, Cholesterol: 60mg, , Sodium: 350mg, Carbohydrates: 15g, Fiber: 2g, Sugar: 2g, Protein: 28g

Tips:

- For even more flavor, add a grated shallot or minced garlic clove to the burger mixture.
- You can substitute ground chicken or lean ground beef for the ground turkey.
- If your burgers are browning too quickly, reduce the air fryer temperature to 375°F (190°C).
- To check for doneness, use a meat thermometer inserted into the thickest part of the burger.
- Serve with your favorite healthy sides, such as air-fried sweet potato fries, a side salad, or roasted vegetables.

Air-Fried Coconut Shrimp

Prep Time: 10 minutes | **Cook Time:** 8-10 minutes | **Total Time**: 18-20 minutes | **Servings:** 4

Ingredients:

- 1 pound large raw shrimp, peeled and deveined with tails on (optional)
- 1/4 cup all-purpose flour
- 1/2 teaspoon garlic powder
- 1/4 teaspoon paprika
- 1/4 teaspoon salt
- 1/4 teaspoon black pepper
- 1 egg, beaten
- 1/2 cup unsweetened shredded coconut
- 1/4 cup panko breadcrumbs
- Cooking spray
- Your favorite dipping sauce (optional)

Instructions:

1. Prep the shrimp: In a small bowl, combine the flour, garlic powder, paprika, salt, and pepper. Toss the shrimp in the flour mixture to coat evenly.
2. Prepare the coating: In a separate bowl, whisk the egg. In another bowl, mix the shredded coconut and panko breadcrumbs.
3. Coat the shrimp: Dip each shrimp in the egg, then roll it in the coconut-panko mixture to coat fully.
4. Preheat the air fryer: Preheat your air fryer to 400°F (200°C).
5. Cook the shrimp: Lightly spray the air fryer basket with cooking spray. Arrange the shrimp in a single layer, ensuring they don't touch. Air fry for 8-10 minutes, flipping halfway through cooking, until golden brown and crispy.
6. Serve: Serve immediately with your favorite dipping sauce, such as sweet chili sauce, sweet and sour sauce, or a citrusy yogurt sauce.

Nutritional Information per serving, estimated: Calories: 250, Fat: 14g, Saturated Fat: 8g, Cholesterol: 150mg, Sodium: 400mg, Carbohydrates: 10g, Fiber: 2g, Sugar: 5g, Protein: 15g

Tips:

- You can use frozen shrimp for convenience, but thaw them completely before coating and cooking.
- For a spicier kick, add a pinch of cayenne pepper to the flour mixture.
- If you don't have panko breadcrumbs, you can use crushed regular breadcrumbs.
- Serve these shrimp with a side of steamed vegetables or brown rice for a complete and healthy meal.
- Make sure not to overcrowd the air fryer basket. Cook the shrimp in batches if necessary.
- The cooking time may vary slightly depending on the size of your shrimp and your air fryer model. Always check for doneness by making sure the shrimp are cooked through and opaque in the center.

Air-Fried Avocado Fries

Cooking Time: 10-12 minutes | **Prep Time**: 10 minutes | **Total Time**: 20-22 minutes | **Servings**: 2-3

Ingredients:

- 1 ripe avocado
- 1/2 cup panko breadcrumbs
- 1/4 cup grated Parmesan cheese (optional)
- 1/4 teaspoon garlic powder
- 1/4 teaspoon onion powder
- 1/4 teaspoon paprika
- Pinch of cayenne pepper (optional)
- Salt and pepper to taste
- Cooking spray

Instructions:

1. Preheat your air fryer to 400°F (200°C).
2. Cut the avocado in half, remove the pit, and peel it. Slice the avocado into 1/2 inch thick wedges.
3. In a shallow bowl, combine the panko breadcrumbs, Parmesan cheese (if using), garlic powder, onion powder, paprika, cayenne pepper (if using), salt, and pepper.
4. Dip each avocado wedge in a beaten egg (optional, for extra crispy coating) and then roll it in the panko mixture, making sure it is evenly coated.
5. Lightly spray the air fryer basket with cooking spray.
6. Arrange the avocado fries in a single layer in the air fryer basket, ensuring they don't touch. Don't overcrowd the basket as this will prevent them from crisping evenly.
7. Air fry for 10-12 minutes, flipping halfway through, until golden brown and crispy.
8. Serve immediately with your favorite dipping sauce, such as sriracha mayo, guacamole, or a light yogurt dip.

Nutritional Information per serving, estimated: Calories: 200-250, Fat: 15-20g, Saturated Fat: 4-5g, Cholesterol: 0mg, Sodium: 100mg, Carbohydrates: 10-15g, Fiber: 4-5g, Sugar: 2-3g, Protein: 2-3g

Tips:

- For a spicier kick, add a pinch of chili powder to the panko mixture.
- If you don't have an air fryer, you can bake the avocado fries in a preheated oven at 400°F (200°C) for 15-20 minutes, flipping them halfway through.
- You can substitute almond flour or another gluten-free flour for the panko breadcrumbs for a gluten-free option.
- To ensure the avocado doesn't brown while prepping, coat the slices in lemon juice or water with a squeeze of lemon.

Air-Fried Turkey Burgers

Prep Time: 10 minutes | **Cook Time**: 12-15 minutes | **Total Time**: 22-27 minutes | **Servings**: 4

Ingredients:

- 1 pound lean ground turkey (90% lean or higher)
- 1/4 cup finely diced onion
- 1/4 cup chopped fresh parsley
- 2 tablespoons Worcestershire sauce
- 1 tablespoon Dijon mustard
- 1 teaspoon dried oregano
- 1/2 teaspoon garlic powder
- 1/2 teaspoon onion powder
- 1/4 teaspoon smoked paprika (optional)
- Salt and black pepper to taste
- 4 hamburger buns
- Your favorite burger toppings (lettuce, tomato, onion, cheese, etc.)

Instructions:

1. **Prep**: Wash and chop the onion and parsley. Preheat your air fryer to 400°F (200°C).
2. **Combine**: In a large bowl, combine the ground turkey, onion, parsley, Worcestershire sauce, Dijon mustard, oregano, garlic powder, onion powder, paprika (if using), salt, and pepper. Gently mix until all ingredients are incorporated, without overworking the meat.
3. **Form Patties**: Divide the mixture into four equal portions and shape each into a burger patty, slightly thicker in the center to prevent them from puffing up too much. Make a shallow indentation in the center of each patty with your thumb.
4. **Air Fry**: Lightly spray the air fryer basket with cooking spray. Place the patties in the basket, ensuring they don't touch. Air fry for 10-12 minutes for medium doneness, or longer for desired doneness (use a meat thermometer to check internal temperature - safe minimum is 165°F). Flip the patties halfway through cooking.
5. **Toast Buns (optional)**: While the burgers cook, you can toast the buns in the air fryer for a minute or two on the "Toast" setting, if your air fryer has one. Alternatively, toast them in a toaster or pan.
6. **Assemble and Serve**: Remove the burgers from the air fryer and let them rest for a few minutes before assembling. Place each burger on a toasted bun and top with your favorite burger fixings. Enjoy!

Nutritional Information per serving: Calories: 250, Fat: 10g, Saturated Fat: 3g, Cholesterol: 50mg, Sodium: 400mg, Carbohydrates: 15g, Fiber: 2g, Sugar: 2g, Protein: 25g

Tips:

- For extra flavor, add a finely grated shallot or cloves of garlic to the mix.
- You can use ground chicken or a blend of ground turkey and chicken for a different flavor profile.
- If your burgers are sticking to the air fryer basket, try spraying them lightly with cooking spray before cooking.
- Serve with air-fried sweet potato fries, zucchini fries, or a side salad for a complete meal.

Air-Fried Brussels Sprouts with Bacon:

Prep Time: 10 minutes | **Cook Time**: 12-15 minutes | **Total Time**: 22-25 minutes | **Servings**: 2-3 (adjust as needed)

Ingredients:

- 1 pound Brussels sprouts, trimmed and halved
- 2-3 slices thick-cut bacon, chopped
- 1 tablespoon olive oil
- 1/2 teaspoon smoked paprika
- 1/4 teaspoon garlic powder
- 1/4 teaspoon onion powder
- Pinch of black pepper
- Optional garnish: Parmesan cheese, balsamic glaze, or lemon zest

Instructions:

1. Preheat your air fryer to 400°F (200°C). Lightly coat the basket with cooking spray if needed.
2. In a large bowl, toss the halved Brussels sprouts with the olive oil, smoked paprika, garlic powder, onion powder, and black pepper until evenly coated.
3. Add the chopped bacon to the bowl with the Brussels sprouts and toss again to combine.
4. Spread the seasoned Brussels sprouts and bacon in a single layer in the air fryer basket, ensuring they don't overlap too much.
5. Air fry for 12-15 minutes, shaking the basket halfway through, or until the Brussels sprouts are tender and lightly browned and the bacon is crispy.
6. Serve immediately with your desired garnish, such as grated Parmesan cheese, a drizzle of balsamic glaze, or a squeeze of lemon zest.

Nutritional Information per serving: Calories: 180, Fat: 10g, Saturated Fat: 3g, Cholesterol: 25mg, Sodium: 200mg, Carbohydrates: 12g, Fiber: 4g, Sugar: 5g, Protein: 7g

Tips:

- For extra crispy Brussels sprouts, cook them for an additional 2-3 minutes.
- You can use turkey bacon for a lighter option.
- Feel free to experiment with other seasonings, such as Italian seasoning, Cajun seasoning, or curry powder.
- Serve these Air-Fried Brussels Sprouts with Bacon as a side dish, appetizer, or snack.
- Air-Fried Potato Skins

Air-Fried Apple Crumble

Prep Time: 15 minutes | **Cook Time**: 12-15 minutes | **Total Time**: 27-30 minutes | **Servings:** 4

Ingredients:

For the Crumble:
- 1/2 cup rolled oats
- 1/4 cup chopped pecans or walnuts
- 2 tablespoons coconut oil, melted
- 1 tablespoon whole wheat flour
- 1/4 teaspoon ground cinnamon
- 1/4 teaspoon ground ginger
- Pinch of sea salt

For the Apples:
- 2-3 apples, peeled, cored, and diced (about 3 cups)
- 1 tablespoon fresh lemon juice
- 1 tablespoon honey or maple syrup
- 1/2 teaspoon ground cinnamon
- Pinch of nutmeg

Instructions:

1. Preheat your air fryer to 375°F (190°C).
2. Make the crumble: In a bowl, combine the rolled oats, chopped nuts, melted coconut oil, flour, cinnamon, ginger, and salt. Mix well until a crumbly mixture forms.
3. Prepare the apples: In another bowl, toss the diced apples with lemon juice, honey or maple syrup, cinnamon, and nutmeg.
4. Assemble the crumble: Divide the apple mixture evenly amongst four small ramekins or oven-safe dishes suitable for your air fryer. Top each portion with the crumble mixture.
5. Air fry: Place the ramekins in the preheated air fryer and cook for 12-15 minutes, or until the apples are tender and the crumble topping is golden brown.
6. Let cool slightly before serving. Enjoy warm with a dollop of Greek yogurt or low-fat whipped cream for an extra treat.

Nutritional Information per serving, estimated: Calories: 250, Fat: 8g, Cholesterol: 0mg, Sodium: 80mg, Carbohydrates: 35g, Fiber: 4g, Protein: 3g

Tips:

- For a vegan option, substitute the honey or maple syrup with agave nectar or date syrup and use vegan butter instead of coconut oil.
- You can add other spices to the crumble mixture, such as cardamom or cloves.
- If your apples are very juicy, you may need to add a tablespoon of oats or flour to the crumble mixture to absorb some of the moisture.
- Don't overcrowd the air fryer basket. Cook the ramekins in batches if necessary.

CHICKEN AND POULTRY RECIPES

Crispy Air Fryer Chicken Wings

Prep Time: 15 minutes | **Cook Time:** 20-25 minutes | **Total Time:** 35-40 minutes | **Servings:** 4

Ingredients:

- 1 pound chicken wings (about 8-10 wings)
- 1 tablespoon vegetable oil
- 1/2 teaspoon paprika
- 1/2 teaspoon garlic powder
- 1/2 teaspoon onion powder
- 1/4 teaspoon black pepper
- 1/4 teaspoon cayenne pepper (optional)
- Salt to taste
- Your favorite wing sauce (optional)

Instructions:

1. Pat the chicken wings dry with paper towels. This helps to ensure crispy skin.
2. In a large bowl, toss the chicken wings with the oil, paprika, garlic powder, onion powder, black pepper, cayenne pepper (if using), and salt. Make sure the wings are evenly coated.
3. Preheat your air fryer to 400°F (200°C).
4. Arrange the chicken wings in a single layer in the air fryer basket, ensuring they don't touch. If your air fryer basket is small, you may need to cook the wings in batches.
5. Air fry for 20-25 minutes, flipping the wings halfway through, until golden brown and crispy. The internal temperature of the wings should reach 165°F (74°C).
6. If desired, toss the cooked wings in your favorite wing sauce for extra flavor.
7. Serve immediately with your favorite dipping sauce, such as blue cheese dressing, ranch dressing, or buffalo sauce.

Nutritional Information per serving: Calories: 350-400, Fat: 25-30g, Saturated Fat: 5-7g, Cholesterol: 100mg, Sodium: 300mg Carbohydrates: 0g, Protein: 30-35g

Tips:

- You can use different spices and seasonings to customize the flavor of your wings. Try using chipotle chili powder, cumin, smoked paprika, or Italian seasoning.
- For extra crispy skin, you can add a tablespoon of baking powder to the seasoning mixture.
- If you don't have an air fryer, you can bake the chicken wings in a preheated oven at 425°F (220°C) for 30-35 minutes, flipping them halfway through
- Be careful not to overcrowd the air fryer basket, as this will prevent the wings from cooking evenly and crisping up. .
- Let the cooked wings rest for a few minutes before serving to allow the juices to redistribute.

Honey Garlic Air Fried Chicken Drumsticks

Prep Time: 15 minutes | **Cook Time**: 20-25 minutes | **Total Time**: 35-40 minutes | **Serving Size:** 4

Ingredients:

- 8 bone-in, skin-on chicken drumsticks
- 1 tablespoon olive oil
- 2 tablespoons soy sauce
- 2 tablespoons honey
- 1 tablespoon minced garlic
- 1 teaspoon grated ginger
- 1/2 teaspoon black pepper
- 1/4 teaspoon red pepper flakes (optional)
- Cooking spray

Instructions:

1. Prep the Chicken: Pat the chicken drumsticks dry with paper towels. Trim any excess fat if desired.
2. Make the Marinade: In a small bowl, whisk together olive oil, soy sauce, honey, garlic, ginger, black pepper, and red pepper flakes (if using).
3. Marinate the Chicken: Place the chicken drumsticks in a large bowl or ziplock bag and pour the marinade over them. Toss to coat evenly. Cover or seal the bag and refrigerate for at least 30 minutes, or up to overnight for deeper flavor.
4. Preheat the Air Fryer: Preheat your air fryer to 400°F (200°C).
5. Air Fry the Chicken: Arrange the chicken drumsticks in a single layer in the air fryer basket, ensuring they don't touch. Lightly spray the drumsticks with cooking spray.
6. Cook and Flip: Air fry for 15 minutes, then flip the drumsticks using tongs. Cook for an additional 5-8 minutes, or until the chicken is cooked through and the internal temperature reaches 165°F (74°C).
7. Glaze and Finish: In a small bowl, whisk together 1 tablespoon of honey and 1 tablespoon of soy sauce. Brush the glaze over the cooked chicken drumsticks in the last 2-3 minutes of cooking for a sticky and flavorful coating.
8. Serve: Enjoy your honey garlic air-fried chicken drumsticks immediately with your favorite dipping sauce, such as sweet and sour sauce, sriracha mayo, or a simple soy sauce-based dipping sauce.

Nutritional Information per serving: Calories: 350, Fat: 20g, Saturated Fat: 5g, Cholesterol: 120mg, Sodium: 500mg, Carbohydrates: 5g, Sugar: 4g, Protein: 30g

Tips:

- For extra crispy skin, pat the chicken drumsticks dry again before air frying.
- If your air fryer tends to cook unevenly, rotate the basket halfway through cooking.
- You can use frozen chicken drumsticks for this recipe, but be sure to add an additional 5-10 minutes to the cooking time.
- To make this recipe gluten-free, use gluten-free soy sauce or coconut aminos.
- For a spicier kick, add more red pepper flakes to the marinade or sprinkle them on the finished chicken drumsticks.

Lemon Herb Air Fryer Chicken Breast

Prep Time: 10 minutes | **Cook Time:** 12-15 minutes | **Total Time:** 22-25 minutes | **Servings**: 2

Ingredients:

- 2 boneless, skinless chicken breasts (about 6-8oz each)
- 1 tablespoon olive oil
- 1 tablespoon lemon juice
- 1 teaspoon dried oregano
- 1/2 teaspoon dried thyme
- 1/4 teaspoon garlic powder
- 1/4 teaspoon salt
- 1/4 teaspoon black pepper
- Fresh parsley, for garnish (optional)

Instructions:

1. Preheat your air fryer to 400°F (200°C).
2. Pat the chicken breasts dry with paper towels.
3. In a small bowl, whisk together olive oil, lemon juice, oregano, thyme, garlic powder, salt, and pepper.
4. Brush the marinade evenly over the chicken breasts, coating both sides.
5. Place the chicken breasts in a single layer in the air fryer basket, ensuring they don't touch.
6. Air fry for 12-15 minutes, or until the chicken is cooked through and reaches an internal temperature of 165°F (74°C).
7. Flip the chicken breasts halfway through cooking for even browning.
8. Garnish with fresh parsley, if desired.

Nutritional Information per serving: Calories: 250, Fat: 8g, Saturated Fat: 2g, Cholesterol: 70mg, Sodium: 200mg, Carbohydrates: 0g, Fiber: 0g, Sugar: 0g, Protein: 35g

Tips:

- You can adjust the amount of herbs and spices to your taste.
- For thicker chicken breasts, add a few extra minutes to the cooking time.
- If you don't have an air fryer, you can bake the chicken in a preheated oven at 400°F (200°C) for 20-25 minutes, or until cooked through.
- Serve with your favorite sides, such as roasted vegetables, mashed potatoes, or rice.

BBQ Ranch Air Fryer Chicken Thighs

Cook Time: 20-25 minutes | **Prep Time**: 10 minutes | **Total Time**: 30-35 minutes | **Servings**: 4

Ingredients:

- 4 boneless, skinless chicken thighs
- 1 tablespoon olive oil
- 1/2 teaspoon paprika
- 1/4 teaspoon garlic powder
- 1/4 teaspoon onion powder
- 1/4 teaspoon black pepper
- 1/4 teaspoon cayenne pepper (optional)
- 1/4 cup BBQ sauce
- 2 tablespoons ranch dressing
- 1/4 cup chopped fresh cilantro (optional)

Instructions:

1. Preheat your air fryer to 400°F (200°C).
2. Pat the chicken thighs dry with paper towels.
3. In a small bowl, whisk together the olive oil, paprika, garlic powder, onion powder, black pepper, and cayenne pepper (if using).
4. Brush the chicken thighs with the spice mixture, coating them evenly.
5. In a separate bowl, whisk together the BBQ sauce and ranch dressing.
6. Place the chicken thighs in a single layer in the air fryer basket.
7. Brush the chicken thighs with the BBQ ranch sauce.
8. Air fry for 20-25 minutes, flipping the chicken thighs halfway through, until cooked through and golden brown. The internal temperature of the chicken should reach 165°F (74°C) when measured with a meat thermometer.
9. Garnish with chopped cilantro (optional) and serve immediately.

Nutritional Information per serving: Calories: 350, Fat: 20g, Saturated Fat: 5g, Cholesterol: 120mg, Sodium: 450mg, Carbohydrates: 5g, Fiber: 1g, Sugar: 5g, Protein: 35g

Tips:

- You can use bone-in, skin-on chicken thighs for this recipe, but the cooking time may need to be adjusted.
- If you don't have an air fryer, you can bake the chicken thighs in a preheated oven at 400°F (200°C) for 25-30 minutes, or until cooked through.
- For a spicier flavor, add a pinch of red pepper flakes to the spice mixture.
- Serve these chicken thighs with your favorite sides, such as roasted vegetables, rice, or mashed potatoes.

Parmesan Crusted Air Fried Chicken Tenders

Prep Time: 10 minutes | **Cook Time:** 12-15 minutes | **Total Time**: 22-27 minutes | **Servings:** 4

Ingredients:

- 1 pound boneless, skinless chicken tenders
- 1/4 cup flour
- 1/2 teaspoon paprika
- 1/4 teaspoon garlic powder
- 1/4 teaspoon onion powder
- 1/4 teaspoon black pepper
- 1 egg, beaten
- 1/2 cup grated Parmesan cheese
- 1/4 cup Italian seasoned breadcrumbs
- Cooking spray

Instructions:

1. Prep the chicken: Pat the chicken tenders dry with paper towels.
2. Make the breading: In a shallow bowl, combine flour, paprika, garlic powder, onion powder, and black pepper. In another bowl, whisk the egg. In a third bowl, combine Parmesan cheese and breadcrumbs.
3. Breading the tenders: Dip each tender in the flour mixture, then the egg, and finally, coat evenly with the Parmesan and breadcrumb mixture.
4. Preheat the air fryer: Preheat your air fryer to 400°F (200°C).
5. Cook the tenders: Lightly spray the air fryer basket with cooking spray. Arrange the breaded tenders in a single layer, ensuring they don't touch.
6. Air fry: Cook for 12-15 minutes, flipping the tenders halfway through, until golden brown and crispy. Check for internal temperature with a meat thermometer; it should reach 165°F (74°C) for safe consumption.
7. Serve: Enjoy your tenders immediately with your favorite dipping sauce, like marinara sauce, honey mustard, or ranch dressing.

Nutritional Information per serving: Calories: 240, Fat: 10g, Saturated Fat: 3g, Cholesterol: 50mg, Sodium: 280mg, Carbohydrates: 8g, Fiber: 1g, Sugar: 2g, Protein: 25g

Tips:

- For extra flavor, add a pinch of dried oregano or Italian seasoning to the breading mixture.
- If you don't have an air fryer, you can bake the tenders on a baking sheet lined with parchment paper at 425°F (220°C) for 20-25 minutes, flipping halfway through.
- For a thicker breading, dip the tenders in the egg twice before coating them in the Parmesan and breadcrumb mixture.
- Leftover tenders can be stored in an airtight container in the refrigerator for up to 3 days. Reheat in the air fryer for a few minutes before serving.

Cajun Spiced Air Fryer Turkey Breast

Prep Time: 10 minutes | **Cook** Time: 20-25 minutes | **Total Time**: 30-35 minutes | **Servings**: 4

Ingredients:

- 1 boneless, skinless turkey breast (1-1.5lbs)
- 1 tablespoon olive oil
- 1 tablespoon paprika
- 1 teaspoon garlic powder
- Salt and freshly ground black pepper, to taste
- 1 teaspoon onion powder
- 1/2 teaspoon cayenne pepper (adjust to your spice preference)
- 1/2 teaspoon black pepper
- 1/4 teaspoon dried thyme
- 1/4 teaspoon dried oregano

Instructions:

1. Prepare the Cajun spice rub: In a small bowl, combine olive oil, paprika, garlic powder, onion powder, cayenne pepper, black pepper, thyme, and oregano. Mix well.
2. Season the turkey breast: Pat the turkey breast dry with paper towels. Season generously with salt and pepper. Rub the Cajun spice mixture evenly over the entire surface of the turkey breast.
3. Preheat the air fryer: Preheat your air fryer to 400°F (200°C).
4. Cook the turkey breast: Place the seasoned turkey breast in the air fryer basket. Avoid overcrowding the basket, cook in batches if necessary.
5. Air fry the turkey breast: Cook for 20-25 minutes, flipping halfway through, or until the internal temperature reaches 165°F (74°C) as measured with an instant-read thermometer.
6. Rest and serve: Remove the turkey breast from the air fryer and let it rest for 5-10 minutes before slicing and serving.

Nutritional Information per serving: Calories: 250, Fat: 8g, , Saturated Fat: 2g, Cholesterol: 70mg, Sodium: 350mg, Carbohydrates: 0g, Fiber: 0g, Sugar: 0g, Protein: 35g

Tips:

- For added moisture, drizzle the turkey breast with olive oil before seasoning.
- If you don't have an air fryer, you can bake the turkey breast in a preheated oven at 400°F (200°C) for 25-30 minutes, or until cooked through.
- Serve the turkey breast with your favorite dipping sauce, such as Cajun remoulade or honey mustard.
- You can use this recipe to cook other cuts of turkey, such as turkey thighs or tenderloins. Adjust the cooking time accordingly.

Teriyaki Glazed Air Fried Chicken Skewers

Prep Time: 15 minutes | **Cook Time**: 12-15 minutes | **Total Time**: 27-30 minutes | **Servings**: 4

Ingredients:

- 1 pound boneless, skinless chicken breasts or thighs, cut into 1-inch cubes
- 1/4 cup low-sodium soy sauce
- 1/4 cup mirin (sweet rice wine)
- 2 tablespoons brown sugar
- 8 wooden skewers, soaked in water for 30 minutes (optional)
- 1 tablespoon honey
- 1 tablespoon rice vinegar
- 1 teaspoon grated ginger
- 1 clove garlic, minced
- 1/2 teaspoon black pepper
- 1/4 teaspoon sesame oil (optional)

Instructions:

- In a large bowl, whisk together the soy sauce, mirin, brown sugar, honey, rice vinegar, ginger, garlic, and black pepper. Add the chicken pieces and toss to coat evenly. Cover and marinate for at least 30 minutes, or up to 4 hours for more intense flavor.
- Preheat your air fryer to 400°F (200°C). If using wooden skewers, thread the chicken cubes onto the skewers, leaving some space between each piece.
- In a small bowl, mix the sesame oil (if using) with 1 tablespoon of the teriyaki marinade.
- Arrange the skewers in a single layer in the air fryer basket, ensuring they don't touch.
- Air fry for 12-15 minutes, flipping the skewers halfway through and brushing with the sesame oil mixture during the last few minutes of cooking. Cook until the chicken is cooked through and golden brown, with an internal temperature of 165°F (74°C).
- Serve immediately with additional teriyaki sauce for dipping, roasted vegetables, or brown rice.

Nutritional Information per serving: Calories: 300, Fat: 12g,, Saturated Fat: 3g, Cholesterol: 80mg, Sodium: 450mg, Carbohydrates: 15g, Fiber: 1g, Sugar: 8g, Protein: 30g

Tips:

- You can use boneless, skinless chicken thighs for a richer flavor.
- If you don't have mirin, you can substitute it with dry sherry or sake.
- For a thicker glaze, cook the leftover marinade in a small saucepan over medium heat until it reduces by half.
- Serve with your favorite dipping sauce, such as sweet and sour sauce, chili sauce, or peanut sauce.
- For a vegan option, use tofu or tempeh instead of chicken.

Buffalo Cauliflower and Chicken Bites

Prep Time: 15 minutes | **Cook Time:** 15-20 minutes | **Total Time:** 30-35 minutes | **Serving**s: 4

Ingredients:

For the Cauliflower Bites:
- 1 head of cauliflower, cut Into bite-sized florets
- 1/4 cup all-purpose flour
- 1/4 cup cornstarch
- 1 teaspoon garlic powder
- 1 teaspoon onion powder
- 1/2 teaspoon paprika
- 1/4 teaspoon salt
- 1/4 cup water
- Cooking spray
- 1/2 cup buffalo sauce (your preferred level of heat)

For the Chicken Bites:
- 1 boneless, skinless chicken breast, cut into bite-sized pieces
- 1/4 cup all-purpose flour
- 1/4 cup breadcrumbs
- 1 teaspoon paprika
- 1/2 teaspoon garlic powder
- 1/4 teaspoon onion powder
- 1/4 teaspoon salt
- 1 egg, beaten
- Cooking spray
- 1/2 cup buffalo sauce (your preferred level of heat)

Instructions:

For the Cauliflower Bites:
- Preheat your air fryer to 400°F (200°C).
- In a large bowl, whisk together the flour, cornstarch, garlic powder, onion powder, paprika, and salt. Add the water and whisk until smooth.
- Add the cauliflower florets to the batter and toss to coat.
- Arrange the coated cauliflower florets in a single layer in the air fryer basket, ensuring they don't touch.
- Lightly spray the cauliflower with cooking spray.
- Air fry for 10-12 minutes, flipping halfway through, until golden brown and crispy.
- In a separate bowl, toss the cooked cauliflower with your desired amount of buffalo sauce.

For the Chicken Bites:
- Preheat your air fryer to 400°F (200°C).
- In a shallow bowl, combine the flour, breadcrumbs, paprika, garlic powder, onion powder, and salt.
- In another shallow bowl, whisk the beaten egg.
- Dip each chicken piece in the egg, then coat it in the breadcrumb mixture.
- Arrange the coated chicken pieces in a single layer in the air fryer basket, ensuring they don't touch.
- Lightly spray the chicken with cooking spray.
- Air fry for 10-12 minutes, flipping halfway through, until golden brown and cooked through.
- In a separate bowl, toss the cooked chicken with your desired amount of buffalo sauce.

Nutritional Information per serving: Calories: 280 (cauliflower) / 350 (chicken), Fat: 12g (cauliflower) / 20g (chicken), Saturated Fat: 2g (cauliflower) / 6g (chicken), Cholesterol: 0mg (cauliflower) / 80mg (chicken), Sodium: 450mg (cauliflower) / 500mg (chicken), Carbohydrates: 15g (cauliflower) / 10g (chicken), Fiber: 3g (cauliflower) / 1g (chicken), Sugar: 4g (cauliflower) / 0g (chicken), Protein: 6g (cauliflower) / 30g (chicken)

Tips:
- You can adjust the amount of buffalo sauce to your desired level of spice.
- For a vegan option, omit the chicken bites and use vegan buffalo sauce and vegan cheese dressing.
- You can use different seasonings on the chicken bites, such as Cajun seasoning or taco seasoning.
- If your air fryer has a preheat function, use it to ensure the air fryer is hot before adding the food.
- Don't overcrowd the air fryer basket, as this will prevent the food from cooking evenly.
- Cooking times may vary depending on the size and thickness of your cauliflower florets and chicken pieces.
- Check for doneness by inserting an instant-read thermometer into the thickest part of the chicken. It should reach an internal temperature of 165°F

Italian Herb Marinated Air Fryer Cornish Hens

Prep Time: 15 minutes | **Marinating Time**: 30 minutes (or overnight for deeper flavor) | **Cook Time:** 25-30 minutes | **Total Time:** 45 minutes - 1 hour (depending on marinating time) | **Servings:** 2

Ingredients:

- 2 Cornish hens (1-1.5 pounds each)
- 2 tablespoons olive oil
- 1 tablespoon lemon juice
- 1 teaspoon dried oregano
- 1 teaspoon dried thyme
- Fresh herbs (optional): rosemary sprigs, thyme sprigs
- 1/2 teaspoon garlic powder
- 1/4 teaspoon onion powder
- 1/4 teaspoon salt
- 1/4 teaspoon black pepper

Instructions:

1. Marinate the Cornish hens: In a large bowl, whisk together olive oil, lemon juice, oregano, thyme, garlic powder, onion powder, salt, and pepper. Place the Cornish hens in the bowl and coat them thoroughly with the marinade. Cover and refrigerate for at least 30 minutes, or overnight for best results.
2. Preheat your air fryer: Preheat your air fryer to 400°F (200°C).
3. Prepare the Cornish hens: Remove the Cornish hens from the marinade and pat them dry with paper towels. Truss the hens with kitchen twine if desired (this helps them cook evenly). Optionally, stuff the cavities with fresh herbs like rosemary or thyme for added flavor.
4. Air fry the Cornish hens: Place the Cornish hens in the air fryer basket, breast side up. Cook for 20 minutes, then flip and cook for an additional 10-15 minutes, or until the internal temperature reaches 165°F (74°C) in the thickest part of the thigh. Use a meat thermometer to check for doneness.
5. Rest and serve: Remove the Cornish hens from the air fryer and let them rest for 5 minutes before carving and serving. Enjoy with your favorite dipping sauce or sides.

Nutritional Information per serving: Calories: 350, Fat: 18g, Saturated Fat: 3g, Cholesterol: 90mg, Sodium: 400mg, Carbohydrates: 2g, Fiber: 0g, Sugar: 1g, Protein: 40g

Tips:

- If your Cornish hens are larger than 1.5 pounds each, you may need to increase the cooking time by 5-10 minutes.
- To ensure crispy skin, avoid overcrowding the air fryer basket. Cook the hens in batches if necessary.
- For a spicier kick, add a pinch of red pepper flakes to the marinade.
- You can substitute store-bought Italian seasoning for the individual herbs in the marinade.
- Feel free to experiment with other fresh herbs in the marinade, such as basil, parsley, or sage.

Garlic Butter Air Fried Turkey Meatballs

Prep Time: 15 minutes | **Cook Time**: 12-15 minutes | **Total Time:** 27-30 minutes | **Servings:** 4

Ingredients:

- 1 pound lean ground turkey (90% lean or higher)
- 1/2 cup panko breadcrumbs
- 1/4 cup grated Parmesan cheese
- 1 tablespoon chopped fresh parsley
- 1 teaspoon dried oregano
- 1/2 teaspoon garlic powder
- 1/4 teaspoon onion powder
- 1/4 teaspoon salt
- 1/4 teaspoon black pepper
- 1 large egg
- 2 tablespoons melted butter
- 1 tablespoon minced garlic

Instructions:

1. Preheat your air fryer to 400°F (200°C).
2. In a large bowl, combine the ground turkey, breadcrumbs, Parmesan cheese, parsley, oregano, garlic powder, onion powder, salt, and pepper.
3. Whisk the egg in a separate bowl. Add the egg to the meatball mixture and combine gently with your hands until just incorporated. Do not overmix, as this can make the meatballs tough.
4. Shape the mixture into 12-16 evenly sized meatballs.
5. In a small bowl, combine the melted butter and minced garlic. Brush the meatballs lightly with the garlic butter mixture.
6. Arrange the meatballs in a single layer in your air fryer basket, ensuring they don't touch. You may need to cook in batches depending on the size of your air fryer.
7. Air fry for 12-15 minutes, flipping the meatballs halfway through, until golden brown and cooked through. The internal temperature of the meatballs should reach 165°F (74°C).
8. Serve immediately with your favorite dipping sauce, such as marinara sauce, ranch dressing, or yogurt-based dip.

Nutritional Information per serving: Calories: 250, Fat: 12g, Saturated Fat: 3g, Cholesterol: 50mg, Sodium: 450mg, Carbohydrates: 5g, Fiber: 1g, Sugar: 2g, Protein: 25g

Tips:

- For a lighter option, use ground turkey breast or a mixture of ground turkey and ground chicken.
- You can add other ingredients to the meatballs, such as grated zucchini, chopped fresh onion, or shredded cheese.
- If you don't have panko breadcrumbs, you can use regular breadcrumbs or crushed crackers.
- To make sure the meatballs are cooked through, use a meat thermometer to check the internal temperature.
- Serve these meatballs as an appetizer, snack, or main course.

BEEF AND PORK

Air Fryer Beef Steak with Garlic Butter

Prep Time: 10 minutes | **Cook Time**: 8-12 minutes | **Total Time**: 20-22 minutes | **Servings**: 2

Ingredients:

- 2 (4-ounce) beef steaks (sirloin, ribeye, or New York strip work well)
- 1 tablespoon olive oil
- Salt and freshly cracked black pepper, to taste
- 2 tablespoons unsalted butter, softened
- 2 cloves garlic, minced
- Fresh herbs (optional), such as parsley, thyme, or rosemary

Instructions:

1. Pat the steaks dry with paper towels.
2. Rub the steaks with olive oil and season generously with salt and pepper.
3. Preheat your air fryer to 400°F (200°C).
4. While the air fryer preheats, prepare the garlic butter. In a small bowl, combine the softened butter, minced garlic, and your chosen herbs (if using).
5. Place the seasoned steak(s) in a single layer in the air fryer basket.
6. Air fry for 4-6 minutes per side for medium-rare, or adjust the cooking time depending on your desired doneness. Use a meat thermometer to check the internal temperature: 135°F for rare, 145°F for medium-rare, 160°F for medium-well.
7. Once the steaks are cooked to your liking, remove them from the air fryer and let them rest for 5 minutes on a plate. This allows the juices to redistribute, resulting in a more tender steak.
8. While the steak rests, spoon the garlic butter over the top and let it melt slightly.
9. Slice the steak against the grain and serve immediately, drizzled with any remaining garlic butter.

Nutritional Information per serving: Calories: 350 (based on a 4 oz steak), Fat: 20g, Saturated Fat: 8g, Cholesterol: 80mg, Sodium: 300mg, Carbohydrates: 0g, Fiber: 0g, Sugar: 0g, Protein: 30g

Tips:

- Use steaks that are similar in thickness for even cooking.
- If your steaks are thicker than 1 inch, you may need to adjust the cooking time slightly.
- You can use different herbs in the garlic butter to customize the flavor.
- Serve with roasted vegetables, mashed potatoes, or a salad for a complete meal.

Crispy Pork Belly Bites with Honey Glaze

Prep Time: 15 minutes | **Cook Time:** 15-20 minutes | **Total Time:** 30-35 minutes | **Servings:** 4

Ingredients:

- 1 pound boneless, skinless pork belly, cut into 1-inch cubes
- 1 tablespoon soy sauce
- 1 tablespoon brown sugar
- 1 tablespoon honey
- 1 tablespoon rice vinegar
- 1 tablespoon hoisin sauce
- 1 teaspoon grated ginger
- 1/2 teaspoon garlic powder
- 1/4 teaspoon black pepper
- 1/4 teaspoon sesame oil
- Cooking spray

Instructions:

1. Marinate the pork: In a large bowl, combine the soy sauce, brown sugar, honey, rice vinegar, hoisin sauce, ginger, garlic powder, black pepper, and sesame oil. Add the pork belly cubes and toss to coat evenly. Marinate for at least 30 minutes, or up to overnight for deeper flavor.
2. Preheat the air fryer: Preheat your air fryer to 400°F (200°C).
3. Air fry the pork: Arrange the pork belly cubes in a single layer in the air fryer basket, ensuring they don't touch. Lightly spray with cooking spray.
4. Cook and glaze: Air fry for 10-12 minutes, flipping halfway through. In a small bowl, whisk together 1 tablespoon of the marinade with 1 tablespoon of honey. Brush the glaze over the pork belly during the last 2-3 minutes of cooking for a sticky and caramelized finish.
5. Serve: Once golden brown and crispy, remove the pork belly bites from the air fryer and serve immediately with your favorite dipping sauce, such as sweet and sour sauce, chili sauce, or sriracha mayo.

Nutritional Information per serving: Calories: 350, Fat: 20g, Saturated Fat: 7g, Cholesterol: 80mg, Sodium: 500mg, Carbohydrates: 5g, Sugar: 4g, Protein: 30g

Tips:

- You can use boneless, skin-on pork belly for a different texture, but remove the skin before cutting it into cubes. However, keep in mind that the cooking time may need to be adjusted.
- To make the sauce thicker, cook it in a small saucepan over medium heat until it reduces slightly.
- For a spicier glaze, add a pinch of red pepper flakes to the glaze mixture.
- Serve these bites with toothpicks for easy dipping.

Air Fried Beef Kebabs with Mediterranean Marinade

Prep Time: 15 minutes | **Marinating Time**: 30 minutes | **Cooking Time**: 10-12 minutes | **Total Time**: 45-57 minutes | **Servings**: 4

Ingredients:

For the marinade:
- 1/4 cup extra virgin olive oil
- 2 tablespoons lemon juice
- 1 tablespoon red wine vinegar
- 1 tablespoon minced garlic
- 1 teaspoon dried oregano
- 1/2 teaspoon dried thyme
- 1/4 teaspoon ground cumin
- 1/4 teaspoon salt
- 8 wooden skewers, soaked in water for 30 minutes
- 1/4 teaspoon black pepper

For the kebabs:
- 1 pound lean ground beef (90% lean or higher)
- 1/2 bell pepper, diced (red, yellow, or orange)
- 1/2 red onion, diced
- 10 cherry tomatoes

Instructions:

1. Make the marinade: In a bowl, whisk together olive oil, lemon juice, red wine vinegar, garlic, oregano, thyme, cumin, salt, and pepper.
2. Marinate the beef: Place the ground beef in a large bowl and pour the marinade over it. Use your hands to massage the marinade into the meat, ensuring it is evenly coated. Cover the bowl and refrigerate for at least 30 minutes, or up to overnight.
3. Prepare the skewers: Thread the diced bell pepper, red onion, and cherry tomatoes onto the soaked wooden skewers, alternating them to create colorful kebabs.
4. Form the beef kebabs: Divide the marinated ground beef into 8 equal portions. Shape each portion into an elongated oval around the prepared skewers, ensuring the beef adheres to the vegetables. Press gently to compact the meat.
5. Preheat the air fryer: Preheat your air fryer to 400°F (200°C).
6. Cook the kebabs: Arrange the kebabs in a single layer in the air fryer basket, ensuring they don't touch. Air fry for 10-12 minutes, flipping halfway through, until the beef is cooked through and browned.
7. Serve: Enjoy your Air-Fried Beef Kebabs with Mediterranean Marinade immediately, with your favorite dipping sauce like tzatziki or hummus.

Nutritional Information per serving, estimated: Calories: 350, Fat: 20g, Saturated Fat: 7g, Cholesterol: 70mg, Sodium: 300mg, Carbohydrates: 5g, Fiber: 1g, Sugar: 2g, Protein: 30g

Tips:
- You can substitute ground lamb or chicken for the ground beef in this recipe.
- Add other vegetables to your kebabs, such as zucchini, mushrooms, or eggplant.
- If you don't have wooden skewers, you can use metal skewers. Just be sure to preheat them in the air fryer for a few minutes before adding the kebabs.
- For a smoky flavor, add a smoked paprika to the marinade.
- Serve the kebabs with whole-wheat pita bread or brown rice for a complete meal.

BBQ Pulled Pork Sliders with Tangy Coleslaw

Prep Time: 20 minutes | **Cook Time**: 45-50 minutes | **Total Time**: 1 hour 5-10 minutes | **Servings:** 4-6

Ingredients:

For the Pulled Beef & Pork:
- 1 lb boneless beef chuck roast, trimmed and cubed
- 1 lb boneless pork shoulder, trimmed and cubed
- 1 tablespoon olive oil
- 1 tablespoon Worcestershire sauce
- 1 tablespoon brown sugar
- 1 teaspoon smoked paprika
- 1 teaspoon onion powder
- 1 teaspoon garlic powder
- 1/2 teaspoon chili powder
- 1/4 teaspoon black pepper
- 1/2 cup beef broth
- 1/4 cup apple cider vinegar

For the Tangy Coleslaw:
- 3 cups shredded green cabbage
- 1 cup shredded red cabbage
- 1/2 cup shredded carrot
- 1/4 cup chopped green onion
- 2 tablespoons mayonnaise
- 2 tablespoons apple cider vinegar
- 1 tablespoon Dijon mustard
- 1 tablespoon honey
- 1/2 teaspoon salt
- 1/4 teaspoon black pepper

For the Sliders:
- 6-8 slider buns (brioche, Hawaiian, or potato rolls)
- Your favorite BBQ sauce

Instructions:
1. Prepare the Pulled Beef & Pork:
2. In a large bowl, combine the beef, pork, olive oil, Worcestershire sauce, brown sugar, paprika, onion powder, garlic powder, chili powder, and black pepper. Toss to coat well.
3. Transfer the mixture to an air fryer basket or baking dish. Pour in the beef broth and apple cider vinegar.
4. Cook in the air fryer at 400°F (200°C) for 45-50 minutes, or until the meat is tender and shreddable. If using a baking dish, cover tightly and bake in a preheated oven at 375°F (190°C) for 2-2.5 hours, or until the meat is tender.
5. Once cooked, shred the meat with two forks, discarding any excess fat.
6. Make the Tangy Coleslaw:
7. In a large bowl, combine the cabbage, carrot, and green onion.
8. In a separate bowl, whisk together the mayonnaise, apple cider vinegar, Dijon mustard, honey, salt, and pepper.
9. Pour the dressing over the vegetables and toss to coat evenly. Refrigerate for at least 30 minutes for the flavors to meld.
10. Assemble the Sliders:
11. Preheat your air fryer to 350°F (175°C) if using.
12. Split the slider buns and lightly toast them in the air fryer for a few minutes, or until slightly golden brown.
13. Divide the pulled beef and pork mixture among the toasted buns. Drizzle with your favorite BBQ sauce.
14. Top each slider with some tangy coleslaw.
15. Serve immediately and enjoy!

Nutritional Information per serving: Calories: 450, Fat: 25g, Saturated Fat: 10g, Cholesterol: 80mg, Sodium: 500mg, Carbohydrates: 30g, Fiber: 2g, Sugar: 10g, Protein: 30g

Tips:
- You can substitute boneless pork loin for the shoulder in this recipe.
- For a spicier coleslaw, add a pinch of red pepper flakes to the dressing.
- If you don't have an air fryer, you can cook the pulled beef and pork in a slow cooker on low for 6-8 hours, or until tender.

Air Fryer Beef Fajitas with Homemade Guacamole

Prep Time: 15 minutes | **Cook Time:** 15 minutes | **Total Time:** 30 minutes | **Servings:** 4

Ingredients:

For the Fajitas:
- 1 lb flank steak, thinly sliced
- 1/2 lb boneless pork shoulder, thinly sliced
- 1 bell pepper, thinly sliced
- 1 onion, thinly sliced
- 2 tablespoons olive oil
- 1 tablespoon fajita seasoning blend
- 1/2 teaspoon smoked paprika
- 1/4 teaspoon cumin
- 1/4 teaspoon chili powder
- Salt and pepper to taste

For the Guacamole:
- 2 ripe avocados, halved and pitted
- 1/2 lime, juiced
- 1/4 cup chopped red onion
- 1/4 cup chopped cilantro
- 1 jalapeno pepper, seeded and finely chopped (optional)
- Salt and pepper to taste

For Serving:
- 8 flour tortillas
- Chopped lettuce, tomato, and shredded cheese (optional)
- Sour cream (optional)

Instructions:

1. Marinate the meat: In a large bowl, combine the beef, pork, olive oil, fajita seasoning, paprika, cumin, chili powder, salt, and pepper. Toss to coat and marinate for at least 15 minutes.
2. Prepare the guacamole: Mash the avocados in a bowl with the lime juice until slightly chunky. Stir in the red onion, cilantro, jalapeno (if using), salt, and pepper. Set aside.
3. Preheat your air fryer to 400°F (200°C).
4. Cook the fajitas: Arrange the beef and pork in a single layer in the air fryer basket, ensuring they don't touch. Cook for 7-8 minutes, flipping halfway through, until cooked through and slightly browned.
5. Cook the vegetables: Add the bell peppers and onions to the air fryer basket with the cooked meat. Cook for 3-4 minutes, stirring occasionally, until softened and slightly charred.
6. Warm the tortillas: Wrap the tortillas in a damp paper towel and microwave for 30 seconds to warm them.
7. Assemble the fajitas: Fill each tortilla with some beef, pork, vegetables, guacamole, and your desired toppings like lettuce, tomato, cheese, and sour cream.

Nutritional Information per serving: Calories: 450, Fat: 20g, Saturated Fat: 8g, Cholesterol: 80mg, Sodium: 500mg, Carbohydrates: 25g, Fiber: 3g, Sugar: 4g, Protein: 40g

Tips:
- You can use skirt steak instead of flank steak for a similar texture.
- Adjust the amount of chili powder to your desired level of spiciness.
- If your air fryer is small, cook the meat and vegetables in batches to avoid overcrowding.
- For a vegetarian option, replace the meat with portobello mushrooms, tofu, or black beans.
- Leftover fajita filling can be stored in the refrigerator for up to 3 days.

Teriyaki Glazed Pork Tenderloin Medallions

Prep Time: 10 minutes | **Cook Time:** 12-15 minutes | **Total Time:** 22-27 minutes | **Servings**: 4

Ingredients:

- 1 pound pork tenderloin, trimmed and cut into 1-inch medallions
- 1 tablespoon low-sodium soy sauce
- 1 tablespoon honey
- 1 tablespoon rice vinegar
- 1 tablespoon sriracha sauce (optional, for added heat)
- 1 teaspoon grated ginger
- 1 clove garlic, minced
- 1/2 teaspoon sesame oil
- 1/4 teaspoon black pepper
- Cooking spray

Instructions:

1. In a small bowl, whisk together soy sauce, honey, rice vinegar, sriracha (if using), ginger, garlic, sesame oil, and black pepper.
2. Place the pork medallions in a shallow dish and pour the teriyaki marinade over them. Toss to coat evenly and marinate for at least 10 minutes, or up to 30 minutes for deeper flavor.
3. Preheat your air fryer to 400°F (200°C). Lightly coat the air fryer basket with cooking spray.
4. Arrange the pork medallions in a single layer in the air fryer basket, ensuring they don't touch.
5. Air fry for 12-15 minutes, flipping the medallions halfway through, until cooked through and golden brown. The internal temperature of the pork should reach 145°F (63°C) for safety.
6. Serve immediately with additional teriyaki sauce for dipping, if desired. You can also garnish with sesame seeds, green onions, or fresh ginger for added flavor.

Nutritional Information per serving: Calories: 240, Fat: 12g, Saturated Fat: 5g, Cholesterol: 80mg, Sodium: 500mg, Carbohydrates: 9g, Fiber: 1g, Sugar: 5g, Protein: 28g

Tips:

- You can use store-bought teriyaki sauce instead of making your own marinade. Be sure to choose a low-sodium option for a healthier choice.
- If you don't have an air fryer, you can bake the pork medallions in a preheated oven at 400°F (200°C) for 20-25 minutes, flipping them halfway through.
- Serve these teriyaki glazed pork tenderloin medallions with steamed rice, roasted vegetables, or a side salad for a complete and healthy meal.
- For a low-carb option, use a low-carb sweetener like stevia in the marinade and serve with cauliflower rice or broccoli instead of traditional rice.

Beef and Pork Meatballs with Marinara Sauce

Prep Time: 15 minutes | **Cook Time:** 12-15 minutes | **Total Time:** 27-30 minutes | **Servings:** 4

Ingredients:

For the meatballs:
- 1 pound lean ground beef (90% lean or above)
- 1 pound lean ground pork (90% lean or above)
- 1/2 cup panko breadcrumbs
- 1/4 cup grated Parmesan cheese
- 1/4 cup chopped fresh parsley
- 1 tablespoon chopped fresh onion
- 1 egg, beaten
- 1 teaspoon dried oregano
- 1/2 teaspoon garlic powder
- 1/2 teaspoon salt
- 1/4 teaspoon black pepper

For the marinara sauce:
- 1 (28-ounce) can crushed tomatoes
- 1 tablespoon tomato paste
- 1 teaspoon dried oregano
- 1/2 teaspoon garlic powder
- 1/4 teaspoon onion powder
- Pinch of red pepper flakes (optional)
- Salt and pepper to taste

Instructions:

1. Prepare the meatballs: In a large bowl, combine the ground beef, ground pork, breadcrumbs, Parmesan cheese, parsley, onion, egg, oregano, garlic powder, salt, and pepper. Mix gently with your hands until just combined. Avoid overmixing.
2. Shape the meatballs: Using a tablespoon or a small ice cream scoop, portion the meat mixture into balls, about 1-inch in diameter. Gently roll each ball between your palms to smooth out the surface.
3. Preheat the air fryer: Preheat your air fryer to 400°F (200°C).
4. Cook the meatballs: Arrange the meatballs in a single layer in the air fryer basket, ensuring they don't touch. Air fry for 12-15 minutes, flipping the meatballs halfway through, until cooked through and golden brown.
5. Prepare the marinara sauce: While the meatballs are cooking, in a saucepan, combine the crushed tomatoes, tomato paste, oregano, garlic powder, onion powder, red pepper flakes (if using), salt, and pepper. Bring to a simmer and cook for 10 minutes, stirring occasionally.
6. Serve: Serve the cooked meatballs with the marinara sauce, spooned over or on the side. You can also serve them with your favorite pasta, rice, or vegetables.

Nutritional Information per serving, estimated: Calories: 350, Fat: 20g, Saturated Fat: 8g, Cholesterol: 80mg, Sodium: 400mg, Carbohydrates: 20g, Fiber: 2g, Sugar: 5g, Protein: 30g

Tips:

- For a lighter option, use lean ground turkey or chicken instead of beef and pork.
- You can add other vegetables to the meatball mixture, such as shredded zucchini or carrots.
- If you don't have an air fryer, you can bake the meatballs in a preheated oven at 400°F (200°C) for 20-25 minutes, flipping them halfway through.
- You can adjust the spices in the meatballs and marinara sauce to your liking.
- For a richer flavor, you can brown the meatballs in a skillet with a little olive oil before air frying them.

Air Fried Korean BBQ Beef Ribs

Prep Time: 15 minutes | **Cook Time**: 15-20 minutes | **Total Time**: 30-35 minutes | **Servings**: 4

Ingredients:

- 1.5 pounds bone-in beef short ribs, cut into 1-inch pieces (flanken cut or similar)
- 1/4 cup soy sauce
- 2 tablespoons brown sugar
- 2 tablespoons honey
- 1 tablespoon rice vinegar
- 1 tablespoon minced garlic
- 1 tablespoon grated ginger
- 1 teaspoon sesame oil
- 1/2 teaspoon red pepper flakes (adjust for spice preference)
- 1/4 teaspoon black pepper
- 1 scallion, sliced thinly (for garnish)
- Sesame seeds (for garnish)

Instructions:

1. Marinate: In a large bowl, combine soy sauce, brown sugar, honey, rice vinegar, garlic, ginger, sesame oil, and red pepper flakes.
2. Add the beef short ribs to the marinade and toss to coat evenly. Cover and refrigerate for at least 30 minutes, or up to overnight for deeper flavor.
3. Preheat the air fryer: Preheat your air fryer to 400°F (200°C). Lightly coat the basket with cooking spray.
4. Air-fry the ribs: Remove the ribs from the marinade, shaking off any excess. Arrange the ribs in a single layer in the air fryer basket, ensuring they don't touch.
5. Air-fry for 15-20 minutes, flipping halfway through, until cooked through and slightly charred. If using thicker ribs, adjust cooking time accordingly. Internal temperature should reach 145°F (63°C) for medium-rare or 160°F (71°C) for medium.
6. Rest and serve: Transfer the cooked ribs to a plate and let them rest for 5 minutes before serving. Sprinkle with sliced scallions and sesame seeds for garnish. Serve with steamed rice, kimchi, and your favorite dipping sauce.

Nutritional Information per serving: Calories: 350, Fat: 20g, Saturated Fat: 8g, Cholesterol: 90mg, Sodium: 500mg, Carbohydrates: 5g, Fiber: 1g, Sugar: 4g, Protein: 30g

Tips:

- You can use boneless short ribs for quicker cooking, adjust time accordingly.
- For a thicker glaze, brush the ribs with leftover marinade during the last few minutes of cooking.
- Add other vegetables like bell peppers or onions to the air fryer basket alongside the ribs for a complete meal.
- Adjust the amount of red pepper flakes based on your desired spice level.
- Experiment with different brands of Korean BBQ marinade for diverse flavor profiles.

Honey Mustard Glazed Pork Chops

Prep Time: 10 minutes | **Cook Time:** 12-15 minutes | **Total Time:** 22-27 minutes | **Servings:** 4

Ingredients:

- 4 bone-in pork chops, thick-cut (about 1 inch)
- 1 tablespoon olive oil
- 1/2 teaspoon Dijon mustard
- 1/4 cup honey
- 1 tablespoon soy sauce
- 1 tablespoon apple cider vinegar
- 1/2 teaspoon garlic powder
- 1/4 teaspoon onion powder
- 1/4 teaspoon black pepper
- Salt to taste (optional)
- Fresh parsley, for garnish (optional)

Instructions:

1. Preheat your air fryer to 400°F (200°C).
2. Pat the pork chops dry with paper towels.
3. In a small bowl, whisk together the olive oil, Dijon mustard, honey, soy sauce, apple cider vinegar, garlic powder, onion powder, and black pepper. Season with salt to taste, if desired.
4. Brush the pork chops generously with the glaze on both sides.
5. Arrange the pork chops in a single layer in the air fryer basket, ensuring they don't touch.
6. Air fry for 12-15 minutes, flipping the pork chops halfway through, until cooked through and golden brown. The internal temperature of the pork chops should reach 145°F (63°C) for safety.
7. Serve immediately, garnished with fresh parsley if desired.

Nutritional Information per serving: Calories: 320, Fat: 17g, Saturated Fat: 5g, Cholesterol: 90mg, Sodium: 350mg, Carbohydrates: 5g, Fiber: 1g, Sugar: 4g, Protein: 35g

Tips:

- For thicker pork chops, you may need to increase the cooking time by 3-5 minutes.
- You can also use boneless pork chops for this recipe. Adjust the cooking time accordingly, as boneless chops cook faster.
- For a sweeter glaze, add a touch more honey. For a spicier glaze, add a pinch of cayenne pepper.
- Serve these pork chops with roasted vegetables, mashed potatoes, or rice for a complete meal.

Beef and Pork Stir-Fry with Fresh Vegetables

Prep Time: 10 minutes | **Cook Time**: 15 minutes | **Total Time:** 25 minutes | **Servings:** 2-3

Ingredients:

- 1 tablespoon vegetable oil
- 1/2 pound lean ground beef
- 1/2 pound boneless, skinless pork loin, thinly sliced
- 1 tablespoon soy sauce (low-sodium preferred)
- 1 tablespoon rice vinegar
- 1 teaspoon sesame oil
- 1/2 teaspoon grated ginger
- 1/4 teaspoon garlic powder
- 1 cup broccoli florets
- 1 cup bell peppers (mixed colors), sliced
- 1 cup snow peas
- 1/2 cup chopped onion (optional)
- 1/4 cup cooked rice (optional)
- Freshly ground black pepper, to taste
- Sesame seeds, for garnish (optional)

Instructions:

1. Preheat your air fryer to 400°F (200°C).
2. In a large bowl, combine the ground beef, pork, soy sauce, rice vinegar, sesame oil, ginger, and garlic powder. Mix well to coat the meat.
3. Lightly spray the air fryer basket with cooking spray. Add the beef and pork mixture, spreading it out in a single layer. Cook for 7 minutes, flipping halfway through.
4. Remove the meat from the air fryer and set aside.
5. Add the broccoli, bell peppers, and snow peas to the air fryer basket. Spray with cooking spray and cook for 5 minutes, stirring occasionally.
6. Add the cooked meat back to the air fryer with the vegetables. If using, add the chopped onion and cook for 2-3 minutes more, until the vegetables are crisp-tender and the meat is cooked through.
7. Stir in the cooked rice (if using) and heat through.
8. Season with black pepper to taste. Garnish with sesame seeds (optional).
9. Serve immediately.

Nutritional Information per serving: Calories: 400, Fat: 20g, Saturated Fat: 6g, Cholesterol: 100mg, Sodium: 400mg, Carbohydrates: 15g, Fiber: 3g, Sugar: 5g, Protein: 30g

Tips:

- You can use any type of vegetables you like in this stir-fry. Other good options include carrots, mushrooms, celery, or zucchini.
- For a spicier stir-fry, add a pinch of red pepper flakes to the marinade.
- If you don't have an air fryer, you can cook the stir-fry in a skillet on the stovetop over medium-high heat.
- For a lower-carb option, serve the stir-fry without the rice.
- Serve with your favorite dipping sauce, such as sweet and sour sauce, chili sauce, or peanut sauce.

APPETIZERS AND SNACKS

Crispy Chicken Wings:

Prep Time: 15 minutes | **Cook Time**: 12-15 minutes | **Total Time**: 27-30 minutes | **Servings**: 4

Ingredients:

- 1 pound chicken wings, separated into flats and drumettes (or whole wings, patted dry)
- 1 tablespoon olive oil
- 1 teaspoon paprika
- 1/2 teaspoon garlic powder
- 1/2 teaspoon onion powder
- 1/4 teaspoon cayenne pepper (optional)
- 1/4 teaspoon black pepper
- Salt to taste
- Your favorite dipping sauce (optional)

Instructions:

1. Preheat your air fryer to 400°F (200°C).
2. In a large bowl, toss the chicken wings with olive oil.
3. In a small bowl, combine paprika, garlic powder, onion powder, cayenne pepper (if using), and black pepper. Sprinkle the spice mixture over the chicken wings and toss to coat evenly. Season with salt to taste.
4. Arrange the chicken wings in a single layer in the air fryer basket, ensuring they don't touch.
5. Air fry for 12-15 minutes, flipping the wings halfway through, until golden brown and crispy and cooked through (internal temperature reaches 165°F).
6. Serve immediately with your favorite dipping sauce, such as buffalo sauce, honey mustard, or BBQ sauce.

Nutritional Information per serving: Calories: 400, Fat: 25g, Saturated Fat: 6g, Cholesterol: 130mg, Sodium: 280mg, Carbohydrates: 2g, Fiber: 0g, Sugar: 1g, Protein: 35g

Tips:

- You can marinate the chicken wings for at least 30 minutes or up to overnight for extra flavor.
- For extra crispy wings, pat the chicken wings dry with paper towels before seasoning.
- If your air fryer basket is small, you may need to cook the wings in batches.
- If you don't have an air fryer, you can bake the chicken wings in a preheated oven at 425°F (220°C) for 25-30 minutes, flipping them halfway through.
- For a healthier option, use skinless chicken thighs instead of wings.

Air-Fried Mozzarella Sticks

Prep Time: 10 minutes | **Cook Time**: 8-10 minutes | **Total** Time: 18-20 minutes | **Servings**: 4

Ingredients:

- 1 cup panko breadcrumbs
- 1/4 cup grated Parmesan cheese
- 1/4 teaspoon garlic powder
- 1/4 teaspoon dried oregano
- 1/8 teaspoon salt
- 1/8 teaspoon black pepper
- 2 large eggs, beaten
- 1 tablespoon water
- 1 (12-ounce) package string cheese, cut into 8 sticks
- Cooking spray

Instructions:

1. In a shallow bowl, combine the panko breadcrumbs, Parmesan cheese, garlic powder, oregano, salt, and pepper.
2. In another shallow bowl, whisk together the eggs and water.
3. Dip each mozzarella stick in the egg mixture, then roll it in the breadcrumb mixture to coat evenly.
4. Preheat your air fryer to 400°F (200°C).
5. Lightly spray the air fryer basket with cooking spray.
6. Arrange the mozzarella sticks in a single layer in the air fryer basket, ensuring they don't touch.
7. Air fry for 8-10 minutes, flipping the sticks halfway through, until golden brown and crispy.
8. Serve immediately with your favorite dipping sauce, such as marinara sauce, ranch dressing, or honey mustard.

Nutritional Information per serving: Calories: 250, Fat: 18g, Saturated Fat: 11g, Cholesterol: 30mg, Sodium: 350mg, Carbohydrates: 14g, Fiber: 1g, Sugar: 2g, Protein: 10g

Tips:

- For a thicker coating, dip the mozzarella sticks in the egg mixture twice and then roll them in the breadcrumb mixture twice.
- You can use different types of cheese, such as cheddar or pepper jack, in place of mozzarella.
- If you don't have an air fryer, you can bake the mozzarella sticks in a preheated oven at 425°F (220°C) for 15-20 minutes, flipping them halfway through.
- Serve these mozzarella sticks as an appetizer, snack, or light meal.

Sweet Potato Fries

Cooking Time: 15-20 minutes | **Prep Time**: 10 minutes | **Total Time**: 25-30 minutes | **Servings**: 2-3

Ingredients:

- 2 medium sweet potatoes, peeled and cut into 1/2-inch thick fries
- 1 tablespoon olive oil
- 1/2 teaspoon paprika
- 1/4 teaspoon garlic powder
- 1/4 teaspoon onion powder
- 1/4 teaspoon salt
- 1/4 teaspoon black pepper
- Cooking spray

Instructions:

1. Preheat your air fryer to 400°F (200°C).
2. In a large bowl, toss the sweet potato fries with olive oil, paprika, garlic powder, onion powder, salt, and pepper.
3. Arrange the fries in a single layer in the air fryer basket, ensuring they don't touch.
4. Air fry for 15-20 minutes, flipping the fries halfway through, until golden brown and crispy.
5. Serve immediately with your favorite dipping sauce, such as ketchup, sriracha mayo, or ranch dressing.

Nutritional Information per serving: Calories: 200, Fat: 5g, Saturated Fat: 1g, Cholesterol: 0mg, Sodium: 40mg, Carbohydrates: 35g, Fiber: 4g, Sugar: 10g, Protein: 2g

Tips:

- For extra crispy fries, soak the sweet potato fries in cold water for 30 minutes before drying them thoroughly and tossing them with the seasonings.
- You can use any type of oil you like, such as avocado oil, canola oil, or vegetable oil.
- If you don't have paprika, you can use another spice blend, such as Cajun seasoning or taco seasoning.
- Serve these fries with a variety of dipping sauces for a fun and flavorful snack.

Buffalo Cauliflower Bites:

Prep Time: 15 minutes | **Cook Time:** 12-15 minutes | **Total Time:** 27-30 minutes | **Servings:** 4

Ingredients:

- 1 head of cauliflower, cut into bite-sized florets
- 1 tablespoon olive oil
- 1/2 teaspoon paprika
- 1/4 teaspoon garlic powder
- 1/4 teaspoon onion powder
- 1/4 teaspoon cayenne pepper (adjust to your spice preference)
- Salt and pepper to taste
- 1/2 cup your favorite buffalo sauce (plus extra for dipping)
- Optional toppings: Celery sticks, blue cheese crumbles, ranch dressing

Instructions:

1. Preheat your air fryer to 400°F (200°C).
2. In a large bowl, toss the cauliflower florets with olive oil, paprika, garlic powder, onion powder, cayenne pepper, salt, and pepper.
3. Arrange the cauliflower florets in a single layer in the air fryer basket, ensuring they don't touch.
4. Air fry for 12-15 minutes, flipping the florets halfway through, until golden brown and crispy.
5. In a small bowl, toss the cooked cauliflower with your desired amount of buffalo sauce.
6. Serve immediately with celery sticks, blue cheese crumbles, ranch dressing, and any other desired toppings.

Nutritional Information per serving: Calories: 220, Fat: 9g, Saturated Fat: 2g, Cholesterol: 0mg, Sodium: 250mg, Carbohydrates: 28g, Fiber: 3g, Sugar: 4g, Protein: 5g

Tips:

- For a thicker coating, you can pre-coat the cauliflower florets in a light cornstarch slurry before tossing them with the spices.
- If you don't have an air fryer, you can bake the cauliflower florets in a preheated oven at 400°F (200°C) for 20-25 minutes, flipping them halfway through.
- For a vegan option, use vegan-friendly buffalo sauce and toppings.
- Serve these bites as an appetizer, snack, or light meal.

Air-Fried Onion Rings

Prep Time: 15 minutes | **Cook Time**: 10-12 minutes | **Total Time**: 25-27 minutes | **Servings**: 4

Ingredients:

- 1 large onion, sliced into 1/2-inch rings (separate into individual rings)
- 1 cup all-purpose flour
- 2 eggs, lightly beaten
- 1 cup panko breadcrumbs
- 1/2 teaspoon paprika
- 1/4 teaspoon garlic powder
- 1/4 teaspoon onion powder
- 1/4 teaspoon salt
- 1/4 teaspoon black pepper
- Cooking spray

Instructions:

1. Preheat your air fryer to 400°F (200°C).
2. In three separate bowls, prepare your coating stations: flour, eggs, and a mixture of panko breadcrumbs, paprika, garlic powder, onion powder, salt, and pepper.
3. Dredge each onion ring in the flour, shaking off any excess. Dip it in the eggs, letting any excess drip off. Finally, coat evenly in the panko breadcrumb mixture.
4. Lightly spray the air fryer basket with cooking spray.
5. Arrange the onion rings in a single layer in the air fryer basket, ensuring they don't touch.
6. Air fry for 10-12 minutes, flipping the rings halfway through, until golden brown and crispy.
7. Serve immediately with your favorite dipping sauce, such as ranch dressing, ketchup, or aioli.

Nutritional Information per serving: Calories: 250, Fat: 12g, Saturated Fat: 2g, Cholesterol: 0mg, Sodium: 300mg, Carbohydrates: 24g, Fiber: 3g, Sugar: 5g, Protein: 5g

Tips:

- For extra crispy onion rings, double-dip them in the egg and breadcrumb mixture.
- If you don't have panko breadcrumbs, you can use regular breadcrumbs instead.
- You can add other spices to the breadcrumb mixture, such as cayenne pepper for a kick of heat or Cajun seasoning for a savory flavor.
- If your onion rings are browning too quickly, reduce the cooking temperature to 375°F (190°C).
- Make sure your onion rings are not crowded in the air fryer basket. This will prevent them from cooking evenly.
- To ensure even cooking, consider checking on the onion rings after 8 minutes and adjust the cooking time as needed.

Air-Fried Jalapeño Poppers (Healthy-ish Version)

Prep Time: 15 minutes | **Cook Time:** 10-12 minutes | **Total Time:** 25-27 minutes | **Servings**: 4-6

Ingredients:

- 6-8 medium jalapeño peppers
- 4 oz. reduced-fat cream cheese, softened
- 1/2 cup shredded low-fat cheddar cheese
- 1/4 cup chopped green onion (optional)
- 1/4 cup finely chopped fresh cilantro (optional)
- 1/4 cup panko breadcrumbs
- 1 tablespoon olive oil
- Cooking spra

Directions:

1. Prepare the jalapeños: Wash and dry the jalapeños. Using a sharp knife, carefully cut each pepper in half lengthwise, leaving the stem intact. Wearing gloves is recommended when handling peppers to avoid burning your hands. With a spoon, carefully remove the seeds and membranes from each pepper half, creating a small cavity. Try to minimize cutting into the flesh of the pepper.
2. Make the filling: In a bowl, combine softened cream cheese, shredded cheddar cheese, green onion (if using), and cilantro (if using). Mix well until smooth and creamy. You can adjust the amount of cheddar cheese depending on your desired level of spiciness.
3. Assemble the poppers: Fill each pepper half with the cheese mixture, ensuring it doesn't overflow.
4. Preheat your air fryer to 400°F (200°C).
5. Prepare the coating: In a shallow dish, combine panko breadcrumbs and olive oil. Mix well to coat the breadcrumbs with oil.
6. Coat the poppers: Roll each stuffed pepper half in the panko breadcrumb mixture to coat evenly.
7. Air fry the poppers: Arrange the coated poppers in a single layer in the air fryer basket, ensuring they don't touch. Spray lightly with cooking spray.
8. Air fry for 10-12 minutes, or until the breadcrumbs are golden brown and the cheese is melted and bubbly. Flip the poppers halfway through cooking for even browning.
9. Serve immediately with your favorite dipping sauce, such as ranch dressing, avocado crema, or salsa.

Nutritional Information per serving, estimated: Calories: 180-200, Fat: 10-12g, Saturated Fat: 5-8g, Cholesterol: 20mg, Sodium: 200-250mg, Carbohydrates: 5-8g, Fiber: 1-2g, Sugar: 1-2g, Protein: 5-7g

Tips:

- For a spicier kick: Leave some of the seeds and membranes in the peppers, or add a pinch of cayenne pepper to the filling.
- For a vegan option: Use vegan cream cheese and omit the cheddar cheese. You can also substitute the cheese with mashed black beans or avocado for a healthier twist.
- Serve with fresh herbs like cilantro or parsley for added flavor and garnish.
- Leftovers: Store leftover poppers in an airtight container in the refrigerator for up to 3 days. Reheat them in the air fryer for a few minutes until crispy again.

Air-Fried Coconut Shrimp

Prep Time: 15 minutes | **Cook Time:** 8-10 minutes | **Total Time:** 23-25 minutes | **Servings**: 4

Ingredients:

- 1 pound large shrimp, peeled and deveined, tails on
- 1/2 cup all-purpose flour
- 1/4 teaspoon paprika
- 1/4 teaspoon garlic powder
- 1/4 teaspoon salt
- 1/4 teaspoon black pepper
- 1 large egg, beaten
- 1/2 cup unsweetened shredded coconut
- 1/2 cup panko breadcrumbs
- Cooking spray

Instructions:

1. In a shallow bowl, whisk together the flour, paprika, garlic powder, salt, and pepper.
2. In another shallow bowl, whisk the egg.
3. In a third shallow bowl, combine the coconut and panko breadcrumbs.
4. Dredge each shrimp in the flour mixture, shaking off any excess. Dip in the egg wash, letting any excess drip off. Finally, coat the shrimp in the coconut-panko mixture, pressing gently to adhere.
5. Preheat your air fryer to 400°F (200°C).
6. Lightly spray the air fryer basket with cooking spray. Arrange the shrimp in a single layer, ensuring they don't touch.
7. Air fry for 8-10 minutes, flipping halfway through, until golden brown and cooked through.
8. Serve immediately with your favorite dipping sauce, such as sweet and sour sauce, chili sauce, or mango chutney.

Nutritional Information per serving: Calories: 350, Fat: 18g, Saturated Fat: 9g, Cholesterol: 150mg, Sodium: 400mg, Carbohydrates: 15g, Fiber: 1g, Sugar: 7g, Protein: 20g

Tips:

- You can use medium-sized shrimp if you prefer. Just adjust the cooking time accordingly.
- For a spicier kick, add a pinch of cayenne pepper to the flour mixture.
- If you don't have an air fryer, you can bake the shrimp in a preheated oven at 425°F (220°C) for 15-20 minutes, flipping halfway through.
- For a gluten-free option, use gluten-free flour and panko breadcrumbs.

Loaded Potato Skins

Prep Time: 15 minutes | **Cook Time**: 20-25 minutes | **Total Time**: 35-40 minutes | **Servings**: 4

Ingredients:

- 4 medium baking potatoes
- 1 tablespoon olive oil
- 1/4 teaspoon salt
- 1/4 teaspoon black pepper
- Optional toppings: chives, crumbled cooked sausage, chili, BBQ sauce
- 1/2 cup shredded cheddar cheese
- 1/4 cup chopped cooked bacon
- 1/4 cup chopped green onion
- 2 tablespoons sour cream

Directions:

1. Preheat the air fryer to 400°F (200°C). Scrub and dry the potatoes. Pierce each potato with a fork several times.
2. Rub the potatoes with olive oil and season with salt and pepper. Place them in the air fryer basket, ensuring they don't touch each other.
3. Cook for 20-25 minutes, flipping halfway through, or until tender when pierced with a fork.
4. While the potatoes cook, prepare your toppings. Shred the cheese, chop the bacon and green onion, and prepare any other desired toppings.
5. Let the potatoes cool slightly. Carefully cut each potato in half lengthwise and scoop out the flesh, leaving a 1/4-inch thick shell. Mash the potato flesh in a bowl with a bit of salt and pepper.
6. Fill each potato skin with the mashed potato mixture. Top with shredded cheese, bacon, green onion, and any other desired toppings.
7. Return the potato skins to the air fryer basket. Cook for 3-5 minutes, or until the cheese is melted and bubbly.
8. Serve immediately with sour cream and any additional toppings.

Nutritional Information approximate per serving: Calories: 350, Fat: 15g, Saturated Fat: 8g, Carbohydrates: 30g, Fiber: 2g, Protein: 10g, Sodium: 300mg

Tips:

- Use Russet potatoes for the best results, as they have a fluffy texture.
- You can bake the potatoes in a traditional oven at 400°F (200°C) for 45-50 minutes before proceeding with the air fryer steps.
- If you don't have an air fryer, you can broil the potato skins under a preheated oven broiler for 3-5 minutes, watching closely to avoid burning.
- Get creative with your toppings! Other options include cooked pulled pork, chili, crumbled blue cheese, salsa, or pico de gallo.

Parmesan Zucchini Fries

Prep Time: 10 minutes | **Cook Time:** 15-20 minutes | **Total Time:** 25-30 minutes | **Servings:** 2-3

Ingredients:

- 2 medium zucchinis (about 1 pound)
- 1 tablespoon olive oil
- 1/2 teaspoon dried oregano
- 1/4 teaspoon garlic powder
- 1/4 teaspoon onion powder
- Salt and pepper to taste
- 1/2 cup panko breadcrumbs
- 1/4 cup grated Parmesan cheese

Instructions:

1. Preheat your air fryer to 400°F (200°C).
2. Wash and trim the ends of the zucchinis. Cut them into thin spears, about 1/4-inch thick and 3-4 inches long.
3. In a bowl, toss the zucchini spears with olive oil, oregano, garlic powder, onion powder, salt, and pepper.
4. In a separate bowl, combine the panko breadcrumbs and Parmesan cheese.
5. Dip each zucchini spear in the breadcrumb mixture, pressing gently to coat evenly.
6. Arrange the coated zucchini fries in a single layer in your air fryer basket, ensuring they don't touch.
7. Air fry for 15-20 minutes, flipping halfway through, until golden brown and crispy.
8. Serve immediately with your favorite dipping sauce, such as marinara sauce, ranch dressing, or aioli.

Nutritional Information per serving: Calories: 150-200, Fat: 7-10g, Carbohydrates: 15-20g, Protein: 3-5g, Fiber: 2-3g, Sodium: 200-300mg

Tips:

- You can use a non-stick cooking spray instead of olive oil to coat the zucchini.
- Add other spices to the breadcrumb mixture, such as paprika, red pepper flakes, or Italian seasoning.
- For extra crispy fries, preheat the air fryer for a few minutes before adding the zucchini.
- Don't overcrowd the air fryer basket, as this will prevent the fries from crisping evenly.
- Serve the fries hot for the best texture.

Avocado Egg Rolls:

Cooking Time: 10 minutes | **Prep Time**: 10 minutes | **Total Time**: 20 minutes | **Serving** Size: 4-6

Ingredients:

- 2 ripe avocados, diced
- 1/4 cup diced red onion
- 1/4 cup chopped cherry tomatoes
- 1/4 cup chopped fresh cilantro
- 1 tablespoon lime juice
- 1/2 teaspoon chili powder
- 1/4 teaspoon garlic powder
- 1/4 teaspoon salt
- 1/4 teaspoon black pepper
- 10 egg roll wrappers (wonton wrappers can be substituted)
- Cooking spray

Directions:

1. Prepare the filling: In a medium bowl, combine diced avocado, red onion, cherry tomatoes, cilantro, lime juice, chili powder, garlic powder, salt, and pepper. Gently mix until well combined.
2. Assemble the egg rolls: Lay an egg roll wrapper on a flat surface with a corner pointing towards you. Place a spoonful of the avocado mixture in the center of the wrapper.
3. Fold and seal: Fold the bottom corner of the wrapper over the filling, then fold in the sides. Tightly roll up the wrapper, moistening the end with a little water to seal. Repeat with remaining wrappers and filling.
4. Preheat and Air Fry: Preheat your air fryer to 400°F (200°C). Spray the air fryer basket with cooking spray.
5. Cook the egg rolls: Working in batches, arrange the egg rolls in a single layer in the air fryer basket, ensuring they don't touch. Lightly spray the tops of the egg rolls with cooking spray.
6. Air fry for 8-10 minutes: Flip the egg rolls halfway through cooking for even browning. Cook until golden brown and crispy.
7. Serve and enjoy: Transfer the cooked egg rolls to a plate lined with paper towels to drain any excess oil. Serve immediately with your favorite dipping sauce, such as sriracha mayo, soy sauce, or guacamole.

Nutritional Information per Serving: Calories: 250, Fat: 14g, Carbohydrates: 12g, Fiber: 4g, Protein: 3g, Sodium: 200mg

Tips:

- To prevent browning, add a squeeze of lime juice to the diced avocado while preparing the filling.
- For a spicier kick, add a pinch of cayenne pepper to the filling.
- If you don't have an air fryer, you can deep-fry the egg rolls in hot oil (350°F) for 2-3 minutes per side.
- Leftover egg rolls can be stored in an airtight container in the refrigerator for up to 2 days. Reheat in the air fryer or oven until crispy.

FISH AND SEAFOOD RECIPES

Crispy Air Fryer Fish Fillets

Prep Time: 10 minutes | **Cook Time**: 12-15 minutes | **Total Time**: 25-30 minutes | **Serving Size**: 2-3 people

Ingredients:

- 2 thick-cut fish fillets (cod, tilapia, halibut, etc.)
- 1 tablespoon olive oil
- 1/2 cup all-purpose flour
- 1/2 cup panko breadcrumbs
- 1/4 teaspoon paprika
- 1/4 teaspoon garlic powder
- 1/4 teaspoon onion powder
- 1/4 teaspoon black pepper
- 1/8 teaspoon salt
- 1 egg, beaten
- Cooking spray

Directions:

1. Prep the Fish: Pat the fish fillets dry with paper towels. Drizzle with olive oil and season lightly with salt and pepper.
2. Make the Breading: In a shallow bowl, whisk together flour, paprika, garlic powder, onion powder, black pepper, and salt. In another bowl, beat the egg. In a third bowl, place the panko breadcrumbs.
3. Dredge the Fish: Dredge each fish fillet in the flour mixture, shaking off any excess. Then, dip in the beaten egg, allowing any excess to drip off. Finally, coat evenly in the panko breadcrumbs, pressing gently to adhere.
4. Air Fry: Preheat your air fryer to 400°F (200°C) for 5 minutes. Lightly spray the air fryer basket with cooking spray. Arrange the breaded fish fillets in a single layer, ensuring they don't touch.
5. Cook and Flip: Air fry for 8-10 minutes, or until golden brown and crispy on one side. Carefully flip the fish fillets and cook for an additional 4-5 minutes, or until the internal temperature reaches 145°F (63°C) checked with a meat thermometer.
6. Serve & Enjoy: Remove the fish fillets from the air fryer and let them cool slightly before serving. Enjoy with your favorite dipping sauces like tartar sauce, lemon wedges, or aioli.

Nutritional Information per Serving: Calories: 350, Fat: 15g, Carbs: 15g, Protein: 30g, Sodium: 400mg

Tips:

- For extra crispy fish, double dip the fillets in the egg and breadcrumb mixture.
- Use a variety of seasonings in the breading to customize the flavor. Some options include Old Bay seasoning, Cajun seasoning, or Italian seasoning.
- If your fish fillets are very thin, adjust the cooking time accordingly to avoid overcooking.
- Don't overcrowd the air fryer basket, as this can prevent the fish from cooking evenly and getting crispy. Cook in batches if necessary.
- Leftover fish fillets can be stored in an airtight container in the refrigerator for up to 2 days. Reheat in the air fryer for a few minutes to crisp them up before serving.

Garlic Herb Shrimp Skewers:

Prep Time: 10 minutes | **Cooking Time**: 8-10 minutes | **Total Time**: 20 minutes | **Servings**: 2-3

Ingredients:

- 1 pound raw shrimp, peeled and deveined (size 16-20)
- 2 tablespoons olive oil
- 2 cloves garlic, minced
- 1 tablespoon fresh parsley, chopped
- 1 teaspoon dried oregano
- 1/2 teaspoon dried thyme
- 1/4 teaspoon salt
- 1/4 teaspoon black pepper
- 1/4 cup lemon juice
- 8 wooden skewers, soaked in water for 30 minutes

Instructions:

1. In a large bowl, whisk together olive oil, garlic, parsley, oregano, thyme, salt, pepper, and lemon juice. Add the shrimp and toss to coat evenly.
2. Marinate the shrimp for at least 15 minutes, or up to 30 minutes for deeper flavor.
3. Preheat your air fryer to 400°F (200°C).
4. Thread the shrimp onto the soaked skewers, leaving a little space between each shrimp.
5. Arrange the skewers in a single layer in the air fryer basket, making sure they are not touching.
6. Air fry for 8-10 minutes, or until the shrimp are pink and cooked through. Flip the skewers halfway through cooking for even browning.
7. Serve immediately with your favorite dipping sauce, such as lemon herb mayo, chimichurri sauce, or cocktail sauce.

Nutritional Information per serving: Calories: 200, Protein: 20g, Fat: 8g, Carbs: 2g, Fiber: 0g

Tips:

- For larger shrimp, adjust the cooking time as needed. They may need an extra 2-3 minutes.
- You can use wooden or metal skewers. Just be sure to soak wooden skewers in water for at least 30 minutes before using to prevent them from burning.
- If your air fryer has a small basket, you may need to cook the skewers in batches.
- Feel free to experiment with different herbs and spices to customize the flavor of your skewers.
- For a fun twist, try adding a drizzle of balsamic glaze or sriracha sauce before serving.

Coconut-Crusted Air Fryer Shrimp

Cooking Time: 8 minutes | **Prep Time**: 10 minutes | **Total Time**: 18 minutes | **Serving Size**: 4 servings

Ingredients:

- 1 pound large shrimp, peeled and deveined, tails on (16/20 count)
- 1/2 cup all-purpose flour
- 1 teaspoon paprika
- 1/2 teaspoon garlic powder
- 1/4 teaspoon salt
- 1/4 teaspoon black pepper
- 2 large eggs, beaten
- 1/2 cup unsweetened shredded coconut
- 1/3 cup panko breadcrumbs
- Cooking spray

Directions:

1. Prep the shrimp: Pat the shrimp dry with paper towels.
2. Set up the dredging station: In separate shallow bowls or dishes, prepare the flour mixture (flour, paprika, garlic powder, salt, and pepper), the beaten eggs, and the coconut-panko mixture (combine coconut and panko breadcrumbs).
3. Bread the shrimp: Working one at a time, dredge each shrimp in the flour mixture, shaking off any excess. Dip in the beaten eggs, letting any excess drip off. Finally, coat generously in the coconut-panko mixture, pressing gently to adhere.
4. Preheat the air fryer: Preheat your air fryer to 400°F (200°C).
5. Air fry the shrimp: In batches, arrange the breaded shrimp in a single layer in the air fryer basket, without overcrowding. Spray lightly with cooking spray. Cook for 4-5 minutes per side, flipping halfway through, or until golden brown and cooked through. Be careful not to overcrowd the basket, as this will prevent even cooking and crispness.
6. Serve: Enjoy your coconut-crusted air fryer shrimp hot with your favorite dipping sauce, such as sweet chili sauce, marinara sauce, or a creamy aioli.

Nutritional Information per serving: Calories: 250, Fat: 12g, Saturated Fat: 5g, Cholesterol: 150mg, Sodium: 400mg, Carbohydrates: 10g, Fiber: 1g, Protein: 20g

Tips:

- For extra sweetness, use sweetened shredded coconut in the breading mixture.
- Add a kick of spice by including a pinch of cayenne pepper in the flour mixture.
- If your shrimp are smaller, adjust the cooking time accordingly.
- Serve with a side of pineapple chunks or mango slices for a tropical twist.
- Let the breaded shrimp rest for a few minutes before cooking to allow the breading to set.
- For a richer flavor, use mayonnaise instead of eggs in the dredging process.

Lemon Garlic Air Fryer Salmon

Cooking Time: 10-12 minutes | **Prep Time:** 5 minutes | **Total Time:** 15-17 minutes | **Serving Size:** 2

Ingredients:

- 2 salmon fillets (5-6 oz each), skinless and boneless
- 1 tablespoon olive oil
- 1 tablespoon lemon juice
- 1 teaspoon dried oregano
- 1/2 teaspoon garlic powder
- 1/4 teaspoon salt
- 1/4 teaspoon black pepper
- 1 lemon, sliced

Directions:

1. Preheat your air fryer to 400°F (200°C).
2. Pat the salmon fillets dry with paper towels.
3. In a small bowl, whisk together olive oil, lemon juice, oregano, garlic powder, salt, and pepper.
4. Brush the salmon fillets with the lemon garlic mixture, coating both sides evenly.
5. Place the salmon fillets in the preheated air fryer basket, leaving space between them for even cooking.
6. Air fry for 10-12 minutes, or until the salmon is cooked through and flakes easily with a fork. The internal temperature should reach 145°F (63°C).
7. Garnish with lemon slices and serve immediately.

Nutritional Information per serving: Calories: 350, Fat: 15g, Saturated Fat: 3g, Cholesterol: 70mg, Sodium: 300mg, Carbohydrates: 1g, Protein: 40g

Tips:

- For thicker salmon fillets, increase the cooking time by 2-3 minutes.
- To add a bit of sweetness, drizzle the salmon with honey before air frying.
- You can substitute fresh herbs, such as parsley or dill, for the dried oregano.
- Serve with roasted vegetables, rice, or quinoa for a complete meal.

Cajun Blackened Catfish

Prep Time: 10 minutes | **Cook Time:** 8-10 minutes | **Total Time:** 20 minutes | **Servings:** 2

Ingredients:

- 2 (6-ounce) skinless catfish fillets
- 1 tablespoon olive oil
- 1 tablespoon Cajun seasoning
- 1/2 teaspoon black pepper
- 1/4 teaspoon salt
- Lemon wedges, for serving

Directions:

1. Preheat: Preheat your air fryer to 400°F (200°C).
2. Season the catfish: Pat the catfish fillets dry with paper towels. In a shallow bowl, combine olive oil, Cajun seasoning, black pepper, and salt. Coat the catfish fillets evenly in the spice mixture.
3. Air fry: Place the seasoned catfish fillets in a single layer in the air fryer basket, ensuring they don't touch each other. Air fry for 4-5 minutes per side, or until the fish is cooked through and flakes easily with a fork. The internal temperature should reach 145°F (63°C).
4. Serve: Plate the cooked catfish fillets and immediately squeeze fresh lemon juice over them. Serve with your favorite dipping sauce, such as remoulade or tartar sauce, and enjoy!

Nutritional Information per Serving: Calories: 350, Fat: 15g, Protein: 35g, Carbs: 5g

Tips:

- For a thicker blackening crust, press the coated catfish fillets into additional Cajun seasoning before air frying.
- If your catfish fillets are thicker than 6 ounces, adjust the cooking time accordingly, adding 2-3 minutes per additional inch of thickness.
- Be careful not to overcrowd the air fryer basket as it can hinder even cooking. Cook in batches if necessary.
- To test for doneness, gently insert a fork into the thickest part of the fish. It should flake easily without resistance.
- For a smoky flavor, add a few drops of liquid smoke to the olive oil before coating the catfish.
- Serve with classic Cajun sides like dirty rice, red beans and rice, or coleslaw.

Sesame Ginger Glazed Mahi Mahi:

Cooking Time: 10 minutes | **Prep Time:** 5 minutes | **Total Time:** 15 minutes | **Serving Size:** 2

Ingredients:

- 2 Mahi Mahi fillets (each about 6 oz)
- 1 tablespoon soy sauce (low-sodium preferred)
- 1 tablespoon rice vinegar
- 1 tablespoon toasted sesame seeds, for garnish
- 1 tablespoon honey
- 1 teaspoon sesame oil
- 1/2 teaspoon freshly grated ginger
- 1/4 teaspoon garlic powder
- 1/4 teaspoon black pepper

Directions:

1. Prepare the glaze: In a small bowl, whisk together soy sauce, rice vinegar, honey, sesame oil, ginger, garlic powder, and black pepper.
2. Prep the mahi-mahi: Pat the fish fillets dry with paper towels. Season both sides with salt and pepper.
3. Preheat the air fryer: Preheat your air fryer to 400°F (200°C) for 5 minutes.
4. Coat the fish: Dip each mahi-mahi fillet in the glaze, ensuring both sides are well coated. Let any excess glaze drip off.
5. Air fry the fish: Arrange the coated fillets in a single layer in the air fryer basket, leaving some space between them for even cooking. Air fry for 8-10 minutes, or until the fish is cooked through and flakes easily with a fork.
6. Garnish and serve: Sprinkle the cooked fish with toasted sesame seeds and serve immediately with your favorite sides, such as steamed rice, roasted vegetables, or a fresh salad.

Nutritional Information per serving: Calories: 350, Fat: 12g, Protein: 38g, Carbohydrates: 10g, Sodium: 500mg

Tips:

- For a thicker glaze, simmer the glaze mixture in a small saucepan over medium heat for 2-3 minutes until slightly reduced.
- If you don't have fresh ginger, you can substitute 1/4 teaspoon ground ginger.
- For a spicier glaze, add a pinch of red pepper flakes.
- Make sure your air fryer basket isn't overcrowded, as this can prevent even cooking. Cook the fish in batches if necessary.
- The cooking time may vary slightly depending on the thickness of your fish fillets and your air fryer model. Start checking for doneness at 8 minutes and adjust accordingly.

Lemon Pepper Scallops

Prep Time: 5 minutes | **Cook Time**: 8-10 minutes | **Total Time**: 13-15 minutes | **Servings**: 2

Ingredients:

- 1 pound large sea scallops, cleaned and patted dry
- 2 tablespoons olive oil
- 1 tablespoon lemon zest
- 1 teaspoon freshly cracked black pepper
- 1/2 teaspoon garlic powder
- 1/4 teaspoon salt
- 1/4 teaspoon smoked paprika (optional)
- Lemon wedges, for garnish
- Fresh parsley, chopped, for garnish

Directions:

1. Preheat your air fryer to 400°F (200°C).
2. In a shallow bowl, combine olive oil, lemon zest, black pepper, garlic powder, salt, and paprika (if using). Toss the scallops in the mixture to coat evenly.
3. Arrange the scallops in a single layer in the air fryer basket, ensuring they don't touch. Avoid overcrowding the basket, cook in batches if necessary.
4. Air fry for 8-10 minutes, or until the scallops are golden brown on the outside and opaque throughout. The internal temperature should reach 145°F (63°C) for safe consumption.
5. Transfer the cooked scallops to a plate and garnish with lemon wedges and fresh parsley. Serve immediately with your desired sides, such as roasted vegetables, rice pilaf, or mashed potatoes.

Nutritional Information per serving: Calories: 220, Fat: 9g, Protein: 24g, Carbohydrates: 0g, Fiber: 0g, Sodium: 280mg

Tips:

- For extra crispy scallops, use panko breadcrumbs or almond flour to coat them before air frying.
- To add a creamy touch, drizzle the cooked scallops with melted butter or a light cream sauce before serving.
- You can substitute dried herbs like thyme or oregano for the fresh parsley.
- Make sure your scallops are dry before air frying to ensure even browning.
- Don't overcrowd the air fryer basket, as this will lead to uneven cooking and soggy scallops.
- Cooking time may vary depending on the thickness of your scallops. Monitor them closely and adjust as needed.

Crispy Coconut-Crusted Cod

Cooking Time: 12-15 minutes | **Prep Time**: 5 minutes | **Total Time**: 17-20 minutes | **Serving Size**: 2

Ingredients:
- 2 (6-ounce) cod fillets
- 1/4 cup unsweetened shredded coconut
- 1/2 cup panko breadcrumbs
- 1 tablespoon flour
- 1 egg, beaten
- 1/4 teaspoon paprika
- 1/4 teaspoon garlic powder
- Salt and pepper to taste
- Cooking spray

Directions:

1. Prep the cod: Pat the cod fillets dry with paper towels.
2. Make the coating: In a shallow bowl, combine the coconut, panko breadcrumbs, flour, paprika, garlic powder, salt, and pepper.
3. Set up the breading station: In separate bowls, have the egg and the coconut mixture ready.
4. Bread the cod: Dip each cod fillet first in the egg, ensuring it's fully coated. Then, dredge it in the coconut mixture, pressing gently to adhere the coating.
5. Preheat and Air Fry: Preheat your air fryer to 400°F (200°C). Spray the air fryer basket with cooking spray.
6. Cook the cod: Place the breaded cod fillets in the air fryer basket, ensuring they don't touch each other. Air fry for 12-15 minutes, or until the cod is cooked through and the crust is golden brown and crispy. Flip the cod halfway through cooking if needed.
7. Serve immediately: Enjoy your crispy coconut-crusted cod hot with your favorite dipping sauce, such as sweet chili sauce, mango salsa, or a simple vinaigrette.

Nutritional Information per serving: Calories: 350, Fat: 15g, Saturated Fat: 6g, Cholesterol: 70mg, Sodium: 250mg, Carbohydrates: 10g, Fiber: 1g, Protein: 30g

Tips:

- For a thicker crust, repeat the breading process by dipping the cod in the egg and then the coconut mixture twice.
- To add a touch of sweetness, substitute 1 tablespoon of honey for half of the flour in the coating mixture.
- If you don't have an air fryer, you can bake the cod in a preheated oven at 425°F (220°C) for 15-20 minutes, or until cooked through and crispy.
- Serve the cod with a side of rice, quinoa, or roasted vegetables for a complete meal.

Mediterranean Grilled Octopus:

Prep Time: 15 minutes | **Cooking Time**: 15-20 minutes | **Total Time**: 30-35 minutes | **Serving Size**: 2-3 people

Ingredients:

- 1 medium octopus, cleaned and tentacles separated (about 1.5 pounds)
- 1/4 cup extra virgin olive oil
- 2 tablespoons lemon juice
- 1 tablespoon chopped fresh oregano
- 1 teaspoon smoked paprika
- 1/2 teaspoon garlic powder
- 1/4 teaspoon salt
- 1/4 teaspoon black pepper
- Lemon wedges, for serving
- Fresh herbs (optional, for garnish)

Instructions:

1. Prepare the octopus: If you haven't purchased it pre-cleaned, clean the octopus by removing the beak, internal organs, and ink sac. Rinse the tentacles thoroughly under cold running water.
2. Make the marinade: In a bowl, whisk together olive oil, lemon juice, oregano, paprika, garlic powder, salt, and pepper. Add the octopus tentacles and toss to coat evenly. Marinate for at least 15 minutes, or up to 30 minutes for additional flavor.
3. Preheat the air fryer: Preheat your air fryer to 400°F (200°C).
4. Cook the octopus: Arrange the octopus tentacles in a single layer in the air fryer basket, ensuring they don't overlap. Avoid overcrowding the basket, as this could steam the octopus instead of grilling it.
5. Air fry: Cook the octopus for 10 minutes, then flip the tentacles and cook for an additional 5-10 minutes, or until tender and slightly charred. Be mindful of the cooking time, as overcooking can make the octopus rubbery.
6. Rest and serve: Transfer the cooked octopus to a plate and let it rest for 5 minutes before serving.
7. Garnish and enjoy: Drizzle the octopus with additional olive oil and lemon juice if desired. Garnish with fresh herbs (parsley, dill, or mint) and serve with lemon wedges for squeezing.

Nutritional Information per serving: Calories: 250, Fat: 10g, Protein: 30g, Carbohydrates: 2g

Tips:

- If your octopus is large, you may need to cook it in batches to avoid overcrowding the air fryer basket.
- Be careful not to overcook the octopus, as it can become rubbery. Check for doneness by piercing the thickest part of a tentacle with a fork. It should be tender but not mushy.
- For a deeper smoky flavor, you can add a few drops of liquid smoke to the marinade.
- Serve this Mediterranean Grilled Octopus with your favorite grilled vegetables, salad, or couscous for a complete meal.

Spicy Sriracha Glazed Shrimp

Cooking Time: 10 minutes | **Prep Time:** 5 minutes | **Total Time:** 15 minutes | **Serving Size:** 2-3 people

Ingredients:

- 1 pound large shrimp, peeled and deveined
- 1 tablespoon cornstarch
- 1/2 teaspoon paprika
- 1/4 teaspoon garlic powder
- 1/4 teaspoon salt
- 1/4 teaspoon black pepper
- 2 tablespoons Sriracha sauce
- 1 tablespoon honey
- 1 tablespoon soy sauce
- 1 tablespoon lime juice
- 1 teaspoon vegetable oil

Directions:

1. Preheat your air fryer to 400°F (200°C).
2. Pat the shrimp dry with paper towels. In a bowl, toss the shrimp with cornstarch, paprika, garlic powder, salt, and pepper until evenly coated.
3. In a separate bowl, whisk together Sriracha sauce, honey, soy sauce, and lime juice.
4. Lightly coat the air fryer basket with cooking spray. Arrange the shrimp in a single layer, ensuring they don't touch.
5. Air fry for 5 minutes. Flip the shrimp and cook for an additional 3-4 minutes, or until the shrimp are cooked through and opaque.
6. While the shrimp are cooking, heat the Sriracha glaze in a small saucepan over low heat. Stir until warm and slightly thickened.
7. Transfer the cooked shrimp to a bowl and toss with the warm Sriracha glaze.
8. Serve immediately with your desired sides, such as rice, noodles, or vegetables.

Nutritional Information per serving: Calories: 220, Fat: 8g, Protein: 20g, Carbohydrates: 5g, Sugar: 3g

Tips:

- For a thicker glaze, simmer the Sriracha sauce for a few minutes before tossing with the shrimp.
- Adjust the amount of Sriracha sauce to your desired level of spice.
- Garnish with chopped green onions, sesame seeds, or fresh cilantro for added flavor and texture.
- You can marinate the shrimp in the Sriracha glaze for 15-30 minutes before air frying for even more intense flavor.
- Make sure your shrimp are relatively similar in size for even cooking.
- Don't overcrowd the air fryer basket, as this can lead to uneven cooking.

VEGETARIAN AND VEGAN DISHES

Crispy Air Fryer Falafel

Cooking Time: 15 minutes | **Prep Time**: 15 minutes | **Total Time**: 30 minutes | **Serving Size**: 4-6 servings

Ingredients:

- 1 cup dried chickpeas, soaked overnight
- 1/2 onion, chopped
- 2 cloves garlic, minced
- 1/2 cup fresh parsley, chopped
- 1/4 cup fresh cilantro, chopped
- 1 teaspoon ground cumin
- Optional toppings: pita bread, tahini sauce, hummus, lettuce, tomato, cucumber, onion
- 1/2 teaspoon ground coriander
- 1/4 teaspoon cayenne pepper (optional)
- 1/4 teaspoon baking soda
- Salt and black pepper to taste
- 2 tablespoons olive oil

Directions:

1. Drain and rinse the soaked chickpeas. Pat them dry with a clean towel.
2. Combine the chickpeas, onion, garlic, parsley, cilantro, spices, baking soda, salt, and pepper in a food processor. Pulse until the mixture is finely chopped but not completely smooth. You want some texture in your falafel.
3. Transfer the mixture to a bowl and cover it with plastic wrap. Refrigerate for at least 30 minutes, or up to overnight, to allow the flavors to meld.
4. Preheat your air fryer to 375°F (190°C). Lightly grease the basket with olive oil.
5. Using your hands, shape the falafel mixture into small balls, about 1-inch in diameter. You can use an ice cream scoop for more uniform shaping.
6. Arrange the falafel balls in a single layer in the air fryer basket, ensuring they don't touch. Lightly spray them with olive oil.
7. Air fry the falafel for 12-15 minutes, flipping them halfway through, until golden brown and crispy.
8. Serve immediately with your desired toppings. Enjoy!

Nutritional Information per serving: Calories: 250, Fat: 8g, Saturated Fat: 1.5g, Cholesterol: 0mg, Sodium: 300mg, Carbohydrates: 25g, Fiber: 5g, Sugar: 4g, Protein: 10g

Tips:

- For a more flavorful falafel, toast the cumin and coriander spices in a dry pan for a few minutes before adding them to the food processor.
- If your falafel mixture seems too wet, add a tablespoon of chickpea flour to help it bind together.
- Don't overcrowd the air fryer basket, as this will prevent the falafel from crisping evenly. Cook them in batches if necessary.
- Leftover falafel can be stored in an airtight container in the refrigerator for up to 3 days. Reheat them in the air fryer or oven until crispy.

Stuffed Bell Peppers

Prep Time: 20 minutes | **Cook Time:** 20-25 minutes | **Total Time:** 40-45 minutes | **Servings:** 4

Ingredients:

For Both:
- 4 bell peppers (red, orange, yellow, or a mix)
- **Versions** 1 tablespoon olive oil
- 1/2 onion, diced
- 2 cloves garlic, minced
- 1 cup cooked quinoa or brown rice

Vegetarian Version:
- 1 can (15 oz) black beans, drained and rinsed
- 1 cup corn kernels, frozen or canned
- 1/2 cup shredded cheddar cheese
- 1/4 cup chopped fresh cilantro
- 1 tablespoon taco seasoning
- Salt and pepper to taste

Vegan Version:
- 1 cup lentils, cooked
- 1/2 cup chopped walnuts or pecans
- 1/4 cup nutritional yeast
- 1 tablespoon smoked paprika
- 1 tablespoon soy sauce
- 1/4 cup chopped fresh parsley
- Salt and pepper to taste

Instructions:

1. Prepare the peppers: Wash and halve the bell peppers lengthwise. Carefully remove the seeds and membranes, leaving the bottoms intact. Brush the inside of each pepper with olive oil.
2. Sauté the base: Heat a skillet over medium heat. Add the olive oil, onion, and garlic. Sauté until softened, about 5 minutes.
3. Prepare the filling: For the vegetarian version, combine the cooked quinoa/brown rice, black beans, corn, cheese, cilantro, and taco seasoning in a bowl. Mix well and season with salt and pepper. For the vegan version, combine the cooked quinoa/brown rice, lentils, nuts, nutritional yeast, paprika, soy sauce, and parsley in a bowl. Mix well and season with salt and pepper.
4. Stuff the peppers: Divide the filling evenly among the prepared bell peppers. Fill them generously, but don't overstuff.
5. Air fry: Preheat your air fryer to 375°F (190°C). Arrange the stuffed peppers in a single layer in the air fryer basket. Cook for 20-25 minutes, or until the peppers are softened and the filling is heated through.
6. Enjoy: Serve the stuffed peppers immediately, topped with additional cheese, cilantro, or parsley (optional).

Nutritional Information per serving, vegetarian version: Calories: 350, Fat: 10g, Carbohydrates: 40g, Fiber: 6g, Protein: 15g

Tips:
- For a crispier texture, preheat the air fryer to 400°F (200°C) for the last 5 minutes of cooking.
- You can substitute other vegetables for the corn and beans/lentils, such as chopped mushrooms, zucchini, or spinach.
- Leftover quinoa/brown rice can be used in this recipe.
- If you don't have an air fryer, you can bake the stuffed peppers in a preheated oven at 375°F (190°C) for 30-35 minutes, or until the peppers are softened and the filling is heated through.

Vegetable Spring Rolls:

Cooking Time: 10 minutes | **Prep Time:** 15 minutes | : **Total Time** 25 minutes | **Serving Size:** 4 people (10 spring rolls)

Ingredients:

- 1 tablespoon olive oil
- 1/2 cup thinly sliced onions
- 2 cups shredded cabbage
- 1/4 cup julienned carrots
- 1/4 cup thinly sliced green bell pepper
- 2 tablespoons soy sauce
- 1/2 tablespoon vinegar
- 1 clove garlic, minced
- 1 tablespoon fresh ginger, minced
- 1/4 cup chopped fresh cilantro
- 10 spring roll wrappers (thawed)
- Salt and pepper to taste

Directions:

1. Preheat your air fryer to 400°F (200°C).
2. Prepare the filling: In a large bowl, heat the olive oil over medium heat. Add the onions, cabbage, carrots, and bell pepper. Cook for 5-7 minutes, or until softened.
3. Stir in the soy sauce, vinegar, garlic, ginger, and cilantro. Season with salt and pepper to taste. Remove from heat and let cool slightly.
4. Assemble the spring rolls: Place a spring roll wrapper on a flat surface with a corner pointing towards you. Add about 1-2 tablespoons of the filling to the bottom third of the wrapper.
5. Fold the bottom corner of the wrapper over the filling. Then, fold the left and right sides of the wrapper inwards. Roll the wrapper tightly towards the top corner, moistening the edge with water to seal. Repeat with remaining wrappers and filling.
6. Air fry the spring rolls: Spray the air fryer basket with cooking spray. Arrange the spring rolls in a single layer, ensuring they don't touch. Cook for 8-10 minutes, or until golden brown and crispy, flipping halfway through.
7. Serve immediately with your favorite dipping sauce, such as vegan sweet and sour sauce or chili sauce.

Nutritional Information per serving: Calories: 200, Fat: 5g, Saturated Fat: 1g, Carbohydrates: 25g, Fiber: 2g, Sugar: 5g, Protein: 5g

Tips:

- For a crispier result, use spring roll wrappers made with rice paper instead of wheat flour wrappers.
- You can add other vegetables to the filling, such as shredded mushrooms, zucchini, or chopped celery.
- If you don't have an air fryer, you can bake the spring rolls in a preheated oven at 400°F (200°C) for 15-20 minutes, or until golden brown and crispy.

Vegetarian Portobello Mushroom Burgers:

Prep Time: 10 minutes | **Cook Time**: 15 minutes | **Total Time**: 25 minutes | **Servings:** 2

Ingredients:

- 2 large portobello mushroom caps, cleaned and stems removed
- 1 tablespoon olive oil
- 1/2 teaspoon balsamic vinegar
- 1/4 teaspoon soy sauce
- 1/4 teaspoon Dijon mustard
- 1/4 teaspoon smoked paprika
- Salt and pepper to taste
- 2 slices Swiss cheese (optional)
- Burger buns of your choice
- Toppings of your choice (e.g., lettuce, tomato, onion, avocado, vegan mayo)

Directions:

1. Preheat your air fryer to 400°F (200°C).

2. **Marinate the mushrooms**:
In a small bowl, whisk together olive oil, balsamic vinegar, soy sauce, Dijon mustard, smoked paprika, salt, and pepper. Gently brush the marinade onto both sides of the portobello caps. Let marinate for 10 minutes, if desired.

3. **Air fry the mushrooms:**
Place the portobello caps in the air fryer basket, stem-side down. Cook for 8-10 minutes, or until tender and slightly browned. Flip and cook for an additional 3-5 minutes.

4. **Add cheese (optional):**
If using, top each mushroom with a slice of cheese and cook for an additional minute, or until melted and bubbly.

5. **Assemble the burgers**:
Toast your burger buns if desired. Place a cooked portobello mushroom on each bun. Add your favorite toppings and enjoy!

Nutritional Information per Serving: Calories: 280, Fat: 18g, Carbs: 20g, Protein: 10g, Fiber: 4g

Vegan Portobello Mushroom Burgers:

Prep Time: 10 minutes | **Cook Time**: 15 minutes | **Total Time**: 25 minutes | **Servings**: 2

Ingredients:

- 2 large portobello mushroom caps, cleaned and stems removed
- 1 tablespoon olive oil
- 1/2 teaspoon tamari or liquid aminos
- 1/4 teaspoon balsamic vinegar
- 1/4 teaspoon smoked paprika
- 1/4 teaspoon garlic powder
- Salt and pepper to taste
- 2 slices vegan cheese (optional)
- Burger buns of your choice
- Toppings of your choice (e.g., lettuce, tomato, onion, avocado, vegan mayo)

Directions:

1. Preheat your air fryer to 400°F (200°C).
2. Marinate the mushrooms: In a small bowl, whisk together olive oil, tamari or liquid aminos, balsamic vinegar, smoked paprika, garlic powder, salt, and pepper. Gently brush the marinade onto both sides of the portobello caps. Let marinate for 10 minutes, if desired.
3. Air fry the mushrooms: Follow steps 3-5 from the vegetarian instructions, using vegan cheese if desired.

Nutritional Information per Serving: Calories: 250, Fat: 16g, Carbs: 22g, Protein: 8g, Fiber: 5g

Tips:

- For extra flavor, add a pinch of dried herbs or spices to the marinade, such as oregano, thyme, or rosemary.
- If your portobello mushrooms are large, you may need to cook them in batches in the air fryer.
- Get creative with your toppings! Some other vegan options include hummus, black bean burgers, or marinated tofu.
- Serve your burgers with a side of air-fried fries or sweet potato wedges for a complete meal.

Crispy Tofu Nuggets (Air Fryer)

Prep Time: 15 minutes | **Cook Time**: 10-12 minutes | **Total Time**: 25 minutes | **Servings**: 4

Ingredients:

- 1 block (14 oz) extra firm tofu, drained and pressed
- 1/4 cup chickpea flour or all-purpose flour
- 1/4 cup nutritional yeast
- 1 tablespoon cornstarch
- 1 teaspoon paprika
- oil
- Optional: additional spices like smoked paprika, oregano, or curry powder
- 1/2 teaspoon garlic powder
- 1/4 teaspoon onion powder
- 1/4 teaspoon black pepper
- 1/4 teaspoon cayenne pepper (optional)
- 1/4 cup unsweetened plant milk
- 1 tablespoon olive

Directions:
1. Press the tofu: Wrap the tofu block in a clean kitchen towel and place a heavy object on top for 15-20 minutes to remove excess moisture. This ensures crispier nuggets.
2. Prepare the breading: In a shallow bowl, combine chickpea flour (or all-purpose flour), nutritional yeast, cornstarch, spices, and salt (to taste). In a separate bowl, whisk together the plant milk and olive oil.
3. Cut the tofu: Dice the tofu into bite-sized nuggets, approximately 1 inch cubes.
4. Coat the tofu: Dredge each tofu nugget in the flour mixture, then dip it in the wet mixture, and finally coat it again in the flour mixture. Make sure the coating is even and complete.
5. Preheat the air fryer: Preheat your air fryer to 400°F (200°C).
6. Air fry the nuggets: Arrange the breaded tofu nuggets in a single layer in the air fryer basket, ensuring they don't touch. Air fry for 10-12 minutes, flipping halfway through, or until golden brown and crispy.
7. Serve: Enjoy your Crispy Tofu Nuggets hot with your favorite dipping sauces like ketchup, vegan mayo, sriracha aioli, or sweet and sour sauce.

Nutritional Information per Serving Calories: 220, Fat: 9g, Protein: 15g, Carbohydrates: 14g, Fiber: 2g, Sodium: 300mg

Tips:
- For extra crispy nuggets, spray the breaded tofu lightly with cooking spray before air frying.
- You can bake these nuggets in a preheated oven at 400°F (200°C) for 20-25 minutes, flipping halfway through, if you don't have an air fryer.
- Get creative with different flavor combinations! You can add different spices to the breading mixture, such as smoked paprika, oregano, or curry powder.
- Serve these nuggets with Buddha bowls, salads, sandwiches, wraps, or as a finger food for parties.

Eggplant Parmesan

Prep Time: 20 minutes | **Cook Time:** 20-25 minutes | **Total Time**: 40-45 minutes | **Servings**: 2-3

Ingredients:

For all:
- 1 large eggplant, thinly sliced (about 1/4 inch)
- 1/4 cup flour (all-purpose or gluten-free)
- 1/2 cup panko breadcrumbs
- 1/4 cup grated Parmesan cheese 1/2 teaspoon Italian seasoning
- 1/4 teaspoon salt
- 1/4 teaspoon black pepper
- Marinara sauce of your choice
- Fresh basil leaves, for garnish (optional)

Vegetarian option:
- 1 large egg, beaten

Vegan option:
- 1 tablespoon ground flaxseed
- 3 tablespoons water

Instructions:

1. Prepare the eggplant: Preheat your air fryer to 400°F (200°C). Slice the eggplant into thin rounds and arrange them in a single layer on paper towels. Sprinkle generously with salt and let sit for 10 minutes. This will help draw out excess moisture and ensure crispy results. Pat the eggplant dry with paper towels.
2. Prepare the breading: In three separate shallow dishes, place the flour, the panko breadcrumbs mixed with Parmesan cheese (vegetarian) or nutritional yeast (vegan), and the Italian seasoning, salt, and pepper.
3. Coat the eggplant: Dip each eggplant slice first in the flour, then the egg (vegetarian) or flaxseed "egg" (vegan), and finally the breadcrumb mixture, ensuring even coating.
4. Air fry the eggplant: Lightly spray the air fryer basket with cooking oil. Arrange the breaded eggplant in a single layer, ensuring they don't touch. Air fry for 7-8 minutes per side, or until golden brown and crispy. You may need to cook in batches depending on the size of your air fryer.
5. Assemble the dish: In a baking dish or heat-resistant plate, spread a thin layer of marinara sauce. Top with a layer of cooked eggplant slices. Repeat with marinara sauce and eggplant until all slices are used. Finish with a sprinkle of Parmesan cheese (vegetarian) or nutritional yeast (vegan).
6. Broil (optional): For a melty cheese topping (vegetarian), broil the assembled dish for 2-3 minutes, watching closely to avoid burning.
7. Serve: Garnish with fresh basil leaves (optional) and enjoy!

Nutritional Information per serving:
Vegetarian: Calories: 400, Fat: 15g, Carbs: 40g, Protein: 15g (using egg)
Vegan: Calories: 350, Fat: 10g, Carbs: 40g, Protein: 10g (using flaxseed "egg")

Tips:

- For a lighter option, skip the breading and simply spray the eggplant slices with olive oil before air frying.
- Add a layer of mozzarella cheese between the eggplant and sauce for an extra cheesy experience.
- Experiment with different types of marinara sauce, such as spicy or creamy.
- Serve with a side of pasta, quinoa, or roasted vegetables.

Sweet Potato Tots

Prep Time: 15 minutes | **Cook Time**: 15-20 minutes | **Total Time:** 30-35 minutes | **Servings**: 2-3

Ingredients:

- 2 medium sweet potatoes (about 1 pound total)
- 1 tablespoon olive oil, avocado oil, or vegetable oil
- 1/4 teaspoon sea salt
- 1/4 teaspoon garlic powder
- 1/4 teaspoon onion powder
- 1/8 teaspoon smoked paprika (optional)
- Pinch of black pepper
- Optional toppings: Sea salt, nutritional yeast, vegan sour cream, vegan chili, avocado slices

Instructions:

1. Preheat your air fryer to 400°F (200°C). If using a basket-style air fryer, preheat for at least 3 minutes to ensure even cooking.
2. Wash and scrub the sweet potatoes thoroughly. Peel them if desired, or leave the skin on for extra nutrients.
3. Grate the sweet potatoes using the large holes of a box grater. Alternatively, pulse them in a food processor until they resemble coarse breadcrumbs.
4. Transfer the grated sweet potatoes to a large bowl. Drizzle with the oil and toss to coat evenly.
5. Add the salt, garlic powder, onion powder, smoked paprika (if using), and black pepper. Stir well to combine and season all the grated sweet potatoes.
6. Shape the tots: Using a tablespoon or your hands, form the mixture into small, bite-sized tots. Avoid making them too large, as they will expand slightly during cooking.
7. Arrange the tots in a single layer in the preheated air fryer basket. Leave a little space between them to allow for even airflow and crisping.
8. Air fry for 15-20 minutes, or until the tots are golden brown and crispy on the outside, and tender on the inside. Shake the basket halfway through cooking to ensure even browning.
9. Serve immediately while hot. Sprinkle with additional sea salt, nutritional yeast, or your favorite toppings.

Nutritional Information (Approximate per Serving): Calories: 200-250, Fat: 5-10g, Sodium: 200-300mg, Carbohydrates: 25-30g, Fiber: 4-5g, Vitamin A: High, Vitamin C: High

Tips:

- For extra crispy tots, use less oil, preheat the air fryer for longer, and cook for a few minutes longer.
- If your tots aren't sticking together well, add a small amount of vegan cornstarch or breadcrumbs to the mixture.
- Experiment with different seasonings and spices to customize the flavor to your liking.
- This recipe can easily be doubled or tripled to serve more people. Just adjust the cooking time as needed.
- Leftover tots can be stored in an airtight container in the refrigerator for up to 3 days and reheated in the air fryer for a few minutes until crispy again.

Coconut-Crusted Tofu (Air Fryer Recipe)

Prep Time: 10 minutes | **Cook Time**: 15 minutes | **Total Time:** 25 minutes | **Servings**: 2-3

Ingredients:

For the marinade:
- 1 tbsp tamari or soy sauce (vegan option)
- 1 tbsp lime juice
- 1 tbsp olive oil
- 1 clove garlic, minced
- 1/2 tsp ginger, grated
- 1/4 tsp black pepper

For the coating:
- 1/4 cup cornstarch
- 1/4 cup panko breadcrumbs
- 1/2 cup unsweetened shredded coconut
- 1/4 tsp paprika
- Pinch of salt

Instructions:
1. Press the tofu: Wrap a block of extra-firm tofu in a clean kitchen towel and place it on a plate. Add another plate on top and weigh it down with something heavy, like a pot or books, for 15 minutes.
2. Prepare the marinade: In a bowl, whisk together the tamari, lime juice, olive oil, garlic, ginger, and pepper.
3. Marinate the tofu: Cut the pressed tofu into cubes or triangles and add them to the marinade. Toss to coat evenly and let sit for at least 10 minutes, or up to 30 minutes for deeper flavor.
4. Prepare the coating: In a shallow bowl, combine the cornstarch, panko, coconut, paprika, and salt.
5. Coat the tofu: Dredge each tofu piece in the cornstarch mixture, then dip it in the marinade again, and finally coat it generously in the coconut mixture. Press the coating firmly to adhere.
6. Preheat the air fryer: Preheat your air fryer to 400°F (200°C).
7. Air fry the tofu: Arrange the coated tofu pieces in a single layer in the air fryer basket, ensuring they don't touch. Air fry for 12-15 minutes, flipping halfway through, or until golden brown and crispy.
8. Serve: Enjoy your coconut-crusted tofu hot with your favorite dipping sauce, like sweet chili sauce, peanut sauce, or vegan mayo.

Nutritional Information approximate per serving: Calories: 300, Fat: 15g, Saturated Fat: 5g, Carbohydrates: 15g, Fiber: 2g, Protein: 20g

Tips
- For a spicier dish, add a pinch of cayenne pepper to the marinade or coating.
- You can use a combination of panko breadcrumbs and gluten-free breadcrumbs for the coating.
- If you don't have an air fryer, you can bake the tofu on a baking sheet preheated to 400°F (200°C) for 20-25 minutes, flipping halfway through.
- For a vegan option, use vegan tamari or soy sauce and a plant-based milk in the marinade instead of yogurt.

Vegan Avocado Fries (Air Fryer)

Prep Time: 10 minutes | **Cook Time**: 8-10 minutes | **Total Time**: 18-20 minutes | **Serving Size**: 2-3 people

Nutritional Information per serving: Calories: 200-250, Fat: 15-20g, Carbohydrates: 15-20g, Protein: 2-3g, Fiber: 5-7g, Sodium: 100-150mg

Ingredients:

- 1 ripe avocado, sliced into 1/2-inch thick wedges
- 1/4 cup chickpea flour or all-purpose flour
- 1/2 teaspoon garlic powder
- 1/4 teaspoon paprika
- 1/4 teaspoon salt
- 1/4 teaspoon black pepper
- 1/3 cup unsweetened plant-based milk
- 1/2 cup panko breadcrumbs
- Cooking spray

Instructions:

- Prepare the avocado: Wash and dry the avocado. Cut it in half, remove the pit, and slice it into 1/2-inch thick wedges. Be sure the wedges are similar in size for even cooking.
- Make the coating: In a shallow bowl, combine the chickpea flour, garlic powder, paprika, salt, and pepper. Whisk to combine.
- Dip and coat: In a separate bowl, pour the plant-based milk. Dip each avocado wedge in the flour mixture, coating it evenly. Then, dip the coated wedge in the plant-based milk, followed by a generous coating of panko breadcrumbs.
- Air fry: Preheat your air fryer to 400°F (200°C). Lightly spray the air fryer basket with cooking spray. Arrange the avocado wedges in a single layer, ensuring they don't touch. Air fry for 8-10 minutes, or until golden brown and crispy, flipping halfway through.
- Serve: Enjoy your avocado fries immediately with your favorite dipping sauce, such as vegan sriracha mayo, guacamole, or salsa.

Tips:

- For a smoother batter, blend the chickpea flour with 2 tablespoons of water before mixing with the spices.
- You can substitute panko breadcrumbs with other gluten-free options like almond flour or crushed cornflakes.
- If your avocado is starting to brown, squeeze some lemon juice on it to prevent further browning.
- Cook the avocado fries in batches if your air fryer basket is small.
- Don't overcrowd the basket, as this can prevent the fries from crisping up properly.

Mediterranean Stuffed Zucchini:

Prep Time: 15 minutes | **Cooking Time:** 20 minutes | **Total Time:** 35 minutes | **Serving Size:** 4

Ingredients:

- 2 medium zucchini, halved lengthwise
- 1 tablespoon olive oil
- 1/2 onion, chopped
- 2 cloves garlic, minced
- 1 cup cooked lentils, rinsed
- 1/2 cup chopped bell pepper
- 1/4 cup chopped sun-dried tomatoes
- 1/4 cup chopped fresh parsley
- 1/4 cup crumbled feta cheese (optional, for vegetarian version)
- 1/4 cup panko breadcrumbs
- 1 tablespoon lemon juice
- Salt and pepper to tast

Directions:

1. Preheat your air fryer to 400°F (200°C).
2. Scoop out the flesh from the zucchini halves, leaving about a 1/2-inch border. Chop the flesh and set aside.
3. In a bowl, heat olive oil and sauté onion and garlic for 2-3 minutes. Add lentils, bell pepper, sun-dried tomatoes, and parsley. Cook for another 5 minutes.
4. Stir in lemon juice, salt, and pepper. If using feta cheese, add it now.
5. Fill the zucchini halves with the lentil mixture. Top with breadcrumbs.
6. Air fry for 20 minutes, or until zucchini is tender and breadcrumbs are golden brown.

Nutritional Information per serving: Calories: 250, Fat: 8g, Saturated Fat: 2g, Carbohydrates: 30g, Fiber: 8g, Sugar: 5g, Protein: 12g

Quinoa and Mushroom Stuffed Zucchini

Prep Time: 15 minutes | **Cooking Time**: 20 minutes | **Total Time**: 35 minutes | **Serving Size**: 4

Ingredients:

- 2 medium zucchini, halved lengthwise
- 1 tablespoon olive oil
- 1/2 onion, chopped
- 2 cloves garlic, minced
- 1 cup cooked quinoa, rinsed
- 1/2 cup chopped mushrooms
- 1/4 cup chopped spinach
- 1/4 cup chopped fresh basil
- 1/4 cup nutritional yeast
- 1/4 cup panko breadcrumbs
- 1 tablespoon lemon juice
- Salt and pepper to taste

Directions:

- Preheat your air fryer to 400°F (200°C).
- Scoop out the flesh from the zucchini halves, leaving about a 1/2-inch border. Chop the flesh and set aside.
- In a bowl, heat olive oil and sauté onion and garlic for 2-3 minutes. Add mushrooms and cook for another 5 minutes.
- Stir in quinoa, spinach, basil, nutritional yeast, lemon juice, salt, and pepper.
- Fill the zucchini halves with the quinoa mixture. Top with breadcrumbs.
- Air fry for 20 minutes, or until zucchini is tender and breadcrumbs are golden brown.

Nutritional Information per serving: Calories: 200, Fat: 5g, Saturated Fat: 1g, Carbohydrates: 35g, Fiber: 6g, Sugar: 5g, Protein: 8g

Tips:

- Feel free to adjust the vegetables and spices in both recipes to your liking.
- For a richer flavor, drizzle the stuffed zucchini with additional olive oil or a balsamic glaze before serving.
- If you don't have an air fryer, you can bake the stuffed zucchini in a preheated oven at 400°F (200°C) for 25-30 minutes.

SIDES AND ACCOMPANIMENTS

Crispy Garlic Parmesan Potato Wedges

Prep Time: 10 minutes | **Cook Time**: 20-25 minutes | **Total Time**: 30-35 minutes | **Servings:** 4

Ingredients:

- 2 russet potatoes, scrubbed and cut into wedges
- 1 tablespoon olive oil
- 1/2 teaspoon garlic powder
- 1/2 teaspoon onion powder
- 1/2 teaspoon paprika
- 1/4 teaspoon dried oregano
- 1/4 teaspoon black pepper
- 1/4 cup grated Parmesan cheese
- Salt, to taste (optional)

Directions:

1. Preheat your air fryer to 400°F (200°C).
2. In a large bowl, toss the potato wedges with olive oil.
3. In a small bowl, combine garlic powder, onion powder, paprika, oregano, and black pepper. Sprinkle the seasoning mixture over the potato wedges and toss to coat evenly.
4. Arrange the potato wedges in a single layer in the air fryer basket, ensuring they don't touch.
5. Cook for 20-25 minutes, flipping halfway through cooking, or until tender and golden brown.
6. Sprinkle with Parmesan cheese and serve immediately.

Nutritional Information per serving: Calories: 250, Fat: 8g, Saturated Fat: 2g, Carbohydrates: 35g, Fiber: 3g, Sugar: 2g, Protein: 4g, Sodium: 250mg

Tips:

- For extra crispy wedges, preheat the air fryer for 5 minutes before adding the potatoes.
- If your potatoes are thick, you may need to increase the cooking time by 5-10 minutes.
- You can substitute other herbs and spices for the oregano, such as rosemary or thyme.
- Serve with your favorite dipping sauce, such as ranch dressing, ketchup, or marinara sauce.

Air Fried Asparagus with Lemon Zest

Cooking Time: 10 minutes | **Prep Time:** 5 minutes | **Total Time:** 15 minutes | **Serving Size:** 2-3 servings

Ingredients:

- 1 pound fresh asparagus, trimmed and ends snapped
- 1 tablespoon olive oil
- 1/2 teaspoon salt
- 1/4 teaspoon black pepper
- 1/2 teaspoon garlic powder (optional)
- Zest of 1 lemon
- 1 tablespoon fresh lemon juice

Directions:

1. Preheat your air fryer to 400°F (200°C). If your air fryer requires preheating, consult your manufacturer's instructions.
2. Prepare the asparagus: Wash and trim the asparagus, snapping off the woody ends. Pat them dry with a paper towel.
3. In a large bowl, toss the asparagus with olive oil, salt, pepper, and garlic powder (if using). Ensure each spear is evenly coated.
4. Arrange the asparagus in a single layer in the air fryer basket. Avoid overcrowding, as this will prevent even cooking.
5. Air fry for 8-10 minutes, flipping the asparagus halfway through. Cook until the asparagus is tender-crisp and slightly browned. Exact cooking time may vary depending on the thickness of your asparagus spears.
6. In a small bowl, combine the lemon zest and lemon juice.
7. Once cooked, remove the asparagus from the air fryer and transfer it to a serving plate. Drizzle with the lemon mixture and toss to coat.
8. Serve immediately and enjoy!

Nutritional Information per serving: Calories: 40, Fat: 1g, Carbohydrates: 5g, Fiber: 2g, Sugar: 2g, Protein: 2g

Tips:

- For a richer flavor, add a sprinkle of grated Parmesan cheese before serving.
- You can substitute avocado oil for olive oil.
- If you don't have fresh lemon, you can use 1/2 teaspoon of bottled lemon juice and skip the zest.
- This recipe is easily doubled or tripled to serve more people.
- Leftover air-fried asparagus can be stored in an airtight container in the refrigerator for up to 3 days.

Crispy Air Fryer Zucchini Fries with Marinara Sauce

Cooking Time: 15 minutes | **Prep Time**: 10 minutes | **Total Time**: 25 minutes | **Serving Size**: 2-3 people

Ingredients:

- 1 medium zucchini, washed and trimmed
- 1/2 cup panko breadcrumbs
- 1/4 cup grated Parmesan cheese
- 1/2 teaspoon dried oregano
- Marinara sauce for dipping (store-bought or homemade)
- 1/4 teaspoon garlic powder
- 1/4 teaspoon paprika
- Pinch of salt and pepper
- 1 egg, lightly beaten
- 1 tablespoon olive oil

Directions:

1. Prep the Zucchini: Cut the zucchini lengthwise into 1/4-inch thick sticks. Pat them dry with paper towels to remove excess moisture.
2. Make the Coating: In a shallow bowl, combine breadcrumbs, Parmesan cheese, oregano, garlic powder, paprika, salt, and pepper.
3. Dredge the Zucchini: Dip each zucchini stick in the egg, letting excess drip off. Then, coat evenly in the breadcrumb mixture, pressing gently to adhere.
4. Preheat the Air Fryer: Preheat your air fryer to 400°F (200°C) for 5 minutes.
5. Air Fry the Fries: In a single layer, arrange the zucchini fries in the air fryer basket. Drizzle with olive oil and lightly mist with cooking spray for extra crispness (optional).
6. Cook in Batches: If your air fryer basket is small, cook the fries in batches to avoid overcrowding, which can prevent them from crisping properly.
7. Air Fry for 10-15 minutes: Cook the fries for 10-15 minutes, flipping halfway through, until golden brown and crispy. Adjust the cooking time based on your air fryer's power and the thickness of your fries.
8. Serve Hot: Enjoy the zucchini fries immediately while they're hot and crispy, dipped in your favorite marinara sauce.

Nutritional Information per serving: Calories: 150, Fat: 5g, Carbohydrates: 15g, Fiber: 2g, Sugar: 5g, Protein: 3g

Tips:

- For extra flavor, add a pinch of red pepper flakes to the breadcrumb mixture.
- To make the fries even healthier, bake them in a preheated oven at 425°F (220°C) for 20-25 minutes, flipping halfway through.
- Use different herbs and spices in the breadcrumb mixture for a variety of flavors.
- Serve the fries with other dipping sauces like ranch dressing, honey mustard, or aioli.

Honey Glazed Carrots with Thyme

Prep Time: 10 minutes | **Cook Time**: 15 minutes | **Total Time**: 25 minutes | **Servings**: 4

Ingredients:

- 1 pound carrots, peeled and trimmed
- 1 tablespoon olive oil
- 2 tablespoons honey
- 1 tablespoon Dijon mustard
- 1/2 teaspoon dried thyme
- 1/4 teaspoon salt
- 1/4 teaspoon black pepper
- Fresh thyme sprigs, for garnish (optional)

Instructions:

1. Preheat the air fryer to 400°F (200°C). If your air fryer has a preheat setting, use it. Otherwise, simply run it empty for 3-4 minutes to heat up.
2. Prepare the carrots: Cut the carrots into even sized pieces, such as sticks, rounds, or baby carrots. Aim for bite-sized pieces that cook evenly.
3. Make the glaze: In a small bowl, whisk together olive oil, honey, Dijon mustard, dried thyme, salt, and pepper.
4. Toss the carrots: In a large bowl, toss the carrot pieces with the prepared glaze until evenly coated.
5. Air fry the carrots: Arrange the carrots in a single layer in the air fryer basket, ensuring they don't overlap too much. Air fry for 10-12 minutes, shaking the basket halfway through, or until the carrots are tender and starting to brown.
6. Glaze and serve: Drizzle the carrots with any remaining glaze in the bowl and toss gently to coat. Air fry for an additional 2-3 minutes to further caramelize the glaze.
7. Garnish and enjoy: Serve the hot honey-glazed carrots immediately, garnished with fresh thyme sprigs if desired.

Nutritional Information per serving: Calories: 120, Fat: 4g, Carbohydrates: 18g, Fiber: 3g, Sugar: 12g, Sodium: 100mg

Tips:

- For a richer flavor, use brown sugar instead of honey.
- Add a pinch of red pepper flakes for a touch of heat.
- If your carrots are thick, you may need to air fry them for a few minutes longer.
- Serve alongside roasted chicken, pork, or fish for a complete meal.

Cauliflower Buffalo Bites with Ranch Dressing

Prep Time: 10 minutes | **Cooking Time**: 15 minutes | **Total Time**: 25 minutes | **Servings**: 4-6

Ingredients:

- 1 head cauliflower, cut into bite-sized florets (about 3 cups)
- 1/4 cup all-purpose flour
- 1/4 cup cornstarch
- 1 teaspoon paprika
- 1/2 teaspoon garlic powder
- 1/4 teaspoon onion powder
- 1/4 teaspoon black pepper
- 1/4 teaspoon salt
- 1/4 cup water
- 1/3 cup hot sauce (adjust to your desired heat level)
- 1 tablespoon melted butter or olive oil
- Ranch dressing, for serving

Directions:

1. Preheat your air fryer to 400°F (200°C).
2. In a large bowl, whisk together flour, cornstarch, paprika, garlic powder, onion powder, black pepper, and salt.
3. In a separate bowl, whisk together water and hot sauce.
4. Dip each cauliflower floret in the flour mixture, coating it evenly. Then, dip it in the hot sauce mixture, letting any excess drip off.
5. Arrange the coated cauliflower florets in a single layer in the air fryer basket. Avoid overcrowding, as this will prevent them from crisping evenly. Cook for 10-12 minutes, flipping halfway through, until golden brown and crispy.
6. In a small bowl, whisk together melted butter or olive oil with 1-2 tablespoons of hot sauce (optional, for extra spice). Toss the cooked cauliflower florets in the buffalo sauce mixture.
7. Serve immediately with ranch dressing for dipping. Enjoy!

Nutritional Information per serving: Calories: 150, Fat: 8g, Carbohydrates: 15g, Protein: 4g, Sodium: 300mg

Tips:

- For a thicker batter, add 1-2 tablespoons of milk to the wet mixture.
- If you don't have an air fryer, you can bake the cauliflower bites in a preheated oven at 425°F (220°C) for 20-25 minutes, flipping halfway through.
- Add a drizzle of blue cheese dressing for a tangy twist.
- For a vegan option, use vegan-friendly flour, cornstarch, and ranch dressing. Substitute melted vegan butter or olive oil for the regular butter.
- Leftovers can be stored in an airtight container in the refrigerator for up to 3 days. Reheat in the air fryer or oven until crispy.

Cornbread Stuffed Jalapeños (Air Fryer Version)

Prep Time: 15 minutes | **Cooking Time**: 10-12 minutes | **Total Time**: 25-27 minutes | **Servings:** 4-6

Ingredients:

- 12-15 fresh jalapeños, medium-sized
- 1 cup cornbread stuffing mix (or follow homemade recipe and crumble)
- 1/2 cup shredded cheddar cheese
- 1/4 cup chopped red onion
- 1/4 cup chopped fresh cilantro
- 1 egg, beaten
- 1 tablespoon melted butter
- 1/4 teaspoon cumin
- 1/4 teaspoon chili powder
- Salt and pepper to taste

Directions:

1. Prepare the jalapeños: Wash and dry the jalapeños. Carefully cut them in half lengthwise, wearing gloves if desired. Use a spoon to remove the seeds and membranes, aiming for medium heat (leave some in for more heat). Preheat your air fryer to 400°F (200°C).
2. Make the stuffing: In a bowl, combine cornbread mix, cheese, onion, cilantro, egg, butter, cumin, chili powder, salt, and pepper. Mix well until a slightly wet stuffing forms.
3. Stuff the jalapeños: Fill each jalapeño half with the stuffing, leaving a little space at the top as it expands while cooking.
4. Air fry: Arrange the stuffed jalapeños in a single layer in the air fryer basket, ensuring they don't touch. Air fry for 10-12 minutes, flipping halfway through, until the cornbread is golden brown and cooked through.
5. Serve: Enjoy the jalapeños hot with your favorite dipping sauce, like ranch or sour cream.

Nutritional Information approximate per serving: Calories: 200-250, Fat: 10-15g, Carbohydrates: 20-25g, Protein: 5-7g, Sodium: 200-300mg

Tips:

- For a creamier filling, add 1/4 cup softened cream cheese to the stuffing mixture.
- To add a smoky flavor, use smoked paprika instead of regular paprika.
- Adjust the amount of chili powder depending on your desired spice level.
- Let the stuffed jalapeños cool slightly before serving to avoid burning your mouth.
- For a crispy exterior, brush the jalapeños with melted butter or olive oil before air frying.

Rosemary Garlic Roasted Potatoes

Prep Time: 10 minutes | **Cooking Time**: 20-25 minutes | **Total Time**: 30-35 minutes | **Serving Size:** 4 servings

Ingredients:

- 1 pound small potatoes
- 2 tablespoons olive oil
- 1/2 teaspoon dried rosemary
- 1/4 teaspoon garlic powder
- 1/2 teaspoon salt
- 1/4 teaspoon black pepper

Directions:

1. Preheat your air fryer to 400°F (200°C).
2. In a large bowl, toss the potatoes with olive oil, rosemary, garlic powder, salt, and pepper until evenly coated.
3. Arrange the potatoes in a single layer in the air fryer basket, making sure they are not touching. If necessary, cook in batches to avoid overcrowding.
4. Air fry for 20-25 minutes, or until the potatoes are golden brown and tender, flipping halfway through cooking. Shake the basket gently a few times during cooking to promote even browning.
5. Serve immediately, garnished with additional fresh rosemary (optional).

Nutritional Information per serving: Calories: 220, Fat: 6g, Saturated Fat: 1g, Cholesterol: 0mg, Sodium: 280mg, Carbohydrates: 34g, Fiber: 3g, Sugar: 2g, Protein: 4g

Tips:

- For extra crispy potatoes, parboil them for 5 minutes before seasoning and air frying.
- You can substitute fresh rosemary for dried rosemary by using 1-2 sprigs, chopped.
- Add other seasonings to your taste, such as paprika, thyme, or onion powder.
- Serve these potatoes with your favorite main course, such as roasted chicken, fish, or tofu.

Air Fryer Brussels Sprouts with Balsamic Glaze

Prep Time: 10 minutes | **Cook Time:** 15-20 minutes | **Total Time:** 25-30 minutes | **Servings:** 2-3

Ingredients:

- 1 pound Brussels sprouts, trimmed and halved
- 1 tablespoon olive oil
- 1/2 teaspoon garlic powder
- 1/4 teaspoon salt
- 1/4 teaspoon black pepper
- 2 tablespoons balsamic vinegar
- 1 tablespoon honey (optional)
- Parmesan cheese, for garnish (optional)

Directions:

1. Preheat your air fryer to 400°F (200°C).
2. In a large bowl, toss the Brussels sprouts with olive oil, garlic powder, salt, and pepper until evenly coated.
3. Arrange the Brussels sprouts in a single layer in the air fryer basket, avoiding overcrowding.
4. Air fry for 15-20 minutes, flipping halfway through cooking, or until the sprouts are tender and crispy.
5. While the sprouts are cooking, whisk together balsamic vinegar and honey (if using) in a small saucepan. Bring to a simmer over medium heat and cook for 2-3 minutes, or until slightly thickened.
6. Remove the Brussels sprouts from the air fryer and toss with the balsamic glaze.
7. Serve immediately, garnished with Parmesan cheese (optional).

Nutritional Information per serving: Calories: 120, Fat: 5g, Carbohydrates: 15g, Fiber: 4g, Sugar: 5g, Protein: 3g

Tips:

- For extra crispy sprouts, use a light coating of cooking spray instead of olive oil.
- You can add other seasonings to the sprouts, such as paprika, red pepper flakes, or Italian seasoning.
- For a sweeter glaze, use more honey or brown sugar.
- If you don't have an air fryer, you can roast the Brussels sprouts in a preheated oven at 400°F (200°C) for 20-25 minutes, tossing halfway through.

Sweet and Spicy Maple Glazed Acorn Squash

Prep Time: 15 minutes | **Cook Time**: 25-30 minutes | **Total Time**: 40-45 minutes | **Serving Size**: 2-3

Ingredients:

- 1 acorn squash, halved and seeds removed
- 1 tablespoon olive oil
- 2 tablespoons maple syrup
- 1/2 teaspoon chili powder
- 1/4 teaspoon ground ginger
- 1/4 teaspoon garlic powder
- Pinch of cayenne pepper (optional, adjust to your spice preference)
- Salt and pepper to taste
- Optional toppings: Chopped pecans, crumbled goat cheese, fresh herbs (parsley, thyme)

Directions:

1. Preheat your air fryer to 400°F (200°C).
2. Cut the acorn squash in half and remove the seeds. Cut each half into wedges, about 1/2-inch thick.
3. In a bowl, toss the squash wedges with olive oil, maple syrup, chili powder, ginger, garlic powder, cayenne pepper (if using), salt, and pepper.
4. Arrange the squash wedges in a single layer in your air fryer basket, ensuring they don't overlap.
5. Air fry for 20-25 minutes, flipping the wedges halfway through cooking, until tender and slightly caramelized.
6. Once cooked, drizzle the squash with additional maple syrup (optional) and sprinkle with your desired toppings (chopped pecans, goat cheese, herbs).
7. Serve immediately and enjoy!

Nutritional Information Approximate per serving: Calories: 150, Fat: 5g, Carbohydrates: 25g, Fiber: 5g, Sugar: 15g, Protein: 2g, Sodium: 100mg

Tips:

- For a deeper flavor, drizzle the squash with a touch of balsamic vinegar before air frying.
- If your air fryer is small, you may need to cook the squash in batches.
- The cooking time may vary slightly depending on the thickness of your squash wedges and your air fryer model.

Parmesan Zucchini Chips

Prep Time: 10 minutes | **Cook Time**: 10-12 minutes | **Total Time**: 22 minutes | **Serving Size**: 2-3 people

Ingredients:

- 1 medium zucchini (about 12 ounces)
- 1 tablespoon olive oil
- 1/4 cup grated Parmesan cheese
- 1/4 cup seasoned breadcrumbs (optional)
- 1/4 teaspoon garlic powder
- 1/4 teaspoon dried oregano
- Salt and pepper to taste

Directions:

1. Preheat your air fryer to 400°F (200°C).
2. Wash and dry the zucchini. Trim off the ends and slice the zucchini into thin rounds, about 1/8-inch thick. You can use a mandoline slicer for evenness.
3. In a large bowl, toss the zucchini slices with olive oil. Ensure they are lightly coated but not swimming in oil.
4. In a separate bowl, combine Parmesan cheese, breadcrumbs (if using), garlic powder, and oregano. Season with salt and pepper to taste.
5. Dredge each zucchini slice in the Parmesan mixture. Press gently to ensure the coating adheres well.
6. Arrange the zucchini chips in a single layer in the air fryer basket. Avoid overcrowding, as this will prevent them from crisping evenly.
7. Air fry for 10-12 minutes, or until golden brown and crispy. Flip the chips halfway through cooking for even browning.
8. Let the chips cool slightly before serving. Enjoy them on their own as a healthy snack or pair them with your favorite dip for added flavor.

Nutritional Information per serving: Calories: 75, Fat: 4g, Carbohydrates: 6g, Fiber: 1g, Protein: 4g, Sodium: 150mg

Tips:

- For a spicier kick, add a pinch of red pepper flakes to the Parmesan mixture.
- If you don't have breadcrumbs, you can use crushed pork rinds for a low-carb option.
- Don't overcrowd the air fryer basket. Cook the chips in batches if necessary.
- To test for doneness, carefully lift a chip. It should be crispy and break easily when snapped.
- Store leftover chips in an airtight container in the refrigerator for up to 3 days.

DESSERTS AND SWEET TREATS

Air Fryer Donuts

Prep Time: 15 minutes | **Cooking Time**: 7-8 minutes | **Total Time**: 25-30 minutes | **Servings**: 10-12 donuts

Ingredients:

For the donuts:
- 1/2 cup warm milk (105°F/40°C)
- 1 tablespoon sugar
- 1 1/2 teaspoons active dry yeast
- 3 1/2 cups all-purpose flour, plus extra for dusting
- 1/4 cup granulated sugar
- 1/2 teaspoon salt
- 1 large egg
- 3 tablespoons unsalted butter, melted
- Vegetable oil spray

For the glaze:
- 1 cup powdered sugar
- 2 tablespoons unsalted butter, melted
- 1/4 teaspoon vanilla extract
- 2-3 tablespoons milk

Directions:

1. Activate the yeast: In a small bowl, whisk together the warm milk, 1 tablespoon sugar, and yeast. Let stand for 5-10 minutes, until foamy and active.
2. Prepare the dough: In a large mixing bowl, whisk together 3 cups flour, granulated sugar, and salt. Add the egg, melted butter, and activated yeast mixture. Stir until a shaggy dough forms. Gradually add remaining 1/2 cup flour, 1 tablespoon at a time, until the dough is smooth and elastic (you may not need all the flour).
3. First rise: Turn the dough onto a lightly floured surface and knead for 5-7 minutes, until smooth and springy. Place the dough in a greased bowl, cover with plastic wrap, and let rise in a warm place for 1 hour, or until doubled in size.
4. Shape the donuts: Punch down the dough and roll it out on a lightly floured surface to 1/2-inch thickness. Cut out donuts using a donut cutter or a large round cookie cutter and a smaller round cutter for the centers. Reroll scraps and cut out additional donuts.
5. Second rise: Place the donuts on a lightly floured baking sheet, cover loosely with plastic wrap, and let rise for another 30 minutes.
6. Preheat the air fryer: Preheat your air fryer to 350°F (175°C) for at least 5 minutes. Lightly spray the basket with vegetable oil spray.
7. Cook the donuts: Working in batches, carefully transfer the donuts to the air fryer basket, leaving space between them. Spray the tops lightly with oil spray. Cook for 3-4 minutes per side, or until golden brown and cooked through.
8. Make the glaze: While the donuts cook, whisk together powdered sugar, melted butter, vanilla extract, and milk in a bowl until smooth. Thin the glaze with additional milk if needed, reaching a dipping consistency.
9. Glaze and serve: Let the donuts cool slightly on a wire rack. Dip each warm donut in the glaze, coating both sides. Let the excess glaze drip off and then place the donuts back on the wire rack to set. Enjoy warm!

Nutritional Information per donut: Calories: 200, Fat: 8g, Saturated Fat: 4g, Cholesterol: 30mg, Sodium: 150mg, Carbohydrates: 28g, Sugar: 12g, Protein: 3g

Tips:
- For a richer flavor, add 1/2 teaspoon of ground cinnamon or nutmeg to the dough.
- You can substitute milk chocolate or white chocolate chips for the donut holes.
- Get creative with your glazes! Try adding a splash of coffee, cocoa powder, or fruit extract for different flavors.
- Let the donuts cool slightly before dipping them in the glaze, as the hot glaze can melt quickly.

Apple Pie Egg Rolls

Cooking Time: 8-10 minutes | **Prep Time:** 15 minutes | **Total Time:** 23-25 minutes | **Serving Size:** 8 egg rolls

Ingredients:

- 3 medium apples (Granny Smith or Honeycrisp recommended), peeled and diced
- 2 tablespoons granulated sugar
- 1 teaspoon ground cinnamon
- ½ teaspoon ground nutmeg
- ¼ teaspoon ground cardamom
- 2 tablespoons brown sugar
- 1 tablespoon cornstarch
- 1 tablespoon lemon juice
- 8 egg roll wrappers
- Vegetable oil spray
- Powdered sugar, for dusting (optional)
- Caramel sauce or whipped cream, for serving

Instructions:

1. Prepare the filling: In a medium bowl, combine diced apples, granulated sugar, cinnamon, nutmeg, and cardamom. Toss to coat evenly. Set aside for 10 minutes, allowing the apples to soften slightly.
2. Thicken the filling: In a small bowl, whisk together brown sugar and cornstarch. Add lemon juice to the apple mixture, then stir in the brown sugar mixture. Cook over medium heat, stirring constantly, until the filling thickens and becomes bubbly, about 5 minutes. Remove from heat and let cool slightly.
3. Assemble the egg rolls: Place an egg roll wrapper on a flat surface with a corner facing you. Add about 2 tablespoons of the cooled filling to the center of the wrapper. Fold the bottom corner up over the filling, then fold in the sides. Roll tightly from the bottom towards the top, sealing the end with a dab of water if needed. Repeat with remaining wrappers and filling.
4. Air fry the egg rolls: Preheat your air fryer to 400°F (200°C). Lightly spray the air fryer basket with oil. Arrange the egg rolls in a single layer, ensuring they don't touch. Air fry for 8-10 minutes, flipping halfway through, until golden brown and crispy.
5. Serve and enjoy: Dust with powdered sugar, if desired, and serve warm with caramel sauce or whipped cream.

Nutritional Information per serving: Calories: 220, Fat: 8g, Saturated Fat: 3g, Cholesterol: 30mg, Sodium: 130mg, Carbohydrates: 32g, Sugar: 18g, Fiber: 2g, Protein: 2g

Tips:

- For a richer flavor, add a dollop of softened cream cheese to the filling before rolling.
- To prevent the wrappers from drying out, keep them covered with a damp cloth while assembling.
- Don't overcrowd the air fryer basket, as this will prevent even cooking.
- Adjust the cooking time depending on your air fryer model and desired level of crispness.
- Leftover filling can be used in oatmeal, yogurt, or pancakes.

Chocolate Chip Cookies

Prep Time: 10 minutes | **Cooking Time:** 8-10 minutes | **Total Time:** 20 minutes | **Servings:** 12 cookies

Ingredients:

- 1/2 cup (1 stick) unsalted butter, softened
- 1/2 cup packed light brown sugar
- 1/4 cup granulated sugar
- 1 large egg
- 1 teaspoon pure vanilla extract
- 1 1/4 cups all-purpose flour
- 1/2 teaspoon baking soda
- 1/4 teaspoon salt
- 1 cup semisweet chocolate chips

Directions:

1. Preheat your air fryer to 350°F (175°C). Lightly grease your air fryer basket with cooking spray or brush with oil. Alternatively, line it with parchment paper for easy cleanup.
2. In a large bowl, cream together the softened butter and sugars until light and fluffy. Use an electric mixer on medium speed for about 2 minutes.
3. Beat in the egg and vanilla extract until well combined. Scrape down the sides of the bowl as needed.
4. In a separate bowl, whisk together the flour, baking soda, and salt. Gradually add the dry ingredients to the wet ingredients, mixing until just combined. Do not overmix.
5. Stir in the chocolate chips using a rubber spatula. Ensure they are evenly distributed throughout the dough.
6. Using a tablespoon or cookie scoop, drop rounded balls of dough onto the prepared air fryer basket. Leave about 1 inch of space between each cookie for proper air circulation.
7. Air-fry the cookies for 8-10 minutes, or until golden brown around the edges and slightly set in the center. The exact cooking time may vary depending on your air fryer model. Watch them closely to prevent burning.
8. Remove the cookies from the air fryer and let them cool on a wire rack for a few minutes before serving. Enjoy warm and gooey!

Nutritional Information per cookie: Calories: 250, Fat: 12g, Saturated Fat: 6g, Cholesterol: 35mg, Sodium: 80mg, Carbohydrates: 32g, Sugar: 18g, Protein: 2g

Tips:

- For chewier cookies, bake for 8 minutes. For crispier cookies, bake for 10 minutes.
- You can substitute chopped nuts, white chocolate chips, or other mix-ins for the semisweet chocolate chips.
- If your dough is too sticky, chill it in the refrigerator for 15 minutes before shaping the cookies.
- Don't overcrowd the air fryer basket. Cook the cookies in batches if necessary.
- Let the air fryer preheat fully before baking for even results.
- Serve your cookies warm with a glass of milk or your favorite ice cream.

Banana Fritters

Prep Time: 10 minutes | **Cook Time**: 10 minutes | **Total Time**: 20 minutes | **Servings**: 4

Ingredients:

- 2 ripe bananas, sliced into 1/2-inch rounds
- 1/2 cup all-purpose flour
- 1 tablespoon sugar
- 1 teaspoon ground cinnamon
- 1/4 teaspoon ground nutmeg
- 1/4 teaspoon salt
- 1 large egg, beaten
- 1 tablespoon milk
- Cooking spray

Instructions:

1. In a shallow bowl, whisk together flour, sugar, cinnamon, nutmeg, and salt.
2. In another shallow bowl, whisk together egg and milk.
3. Preheat your air fryer to 400°F (200°C). Lightly coat the air fryer basket with cooking spray.
4. Working one at a time, dip each banana slice in the flour mixture, coating evenly. Shake off any excess flour.
5. Dip the coated banana slice in the egg mixture, then roll in the remaining flour mixture to coat completely.
6. Place the coated banana slices in a single layer in the air fryer basket, ensuring they don't touch.
7. Air fry for 5-7 minutes, or until golden brown and crispy. Flip the fritters halfway through cooking for even browning.
8. Serve warm with your favorite dipping sauce, such as honey, maple syrup, whipped cream, or chocolate sauce.

Nutritional Information per serving: Calories: 200, Fat: 5g, Saturated Fat: 2g, Cholesterol: 25mg, Sodium: 100mg, Carbohydrates: 30g, Sugar: 15g, Fiber: 2g, Protein: 3g

Tips:

- For a gluten-free option, use a gluten-free flour blend.
- To add some extra flavor, sprinkle the banana slices with chopped nuts or dried fruit before coating them in flour.
- If your bananas are very ripe, you may need to adjust the cooking time slightly, as they may cook faster.
- Make sure your air fryer is preheated before adding the fritters, for optimal crisping.

Air Fryer Churros

Prep Time: 15 minutes, Cooking Time: 15-20 minutes, Total Time: 35 minutes, Serving Size: 6-8 churros

Ingredients:

- 1/2 cup water
- 1/3 cup unsalted butter, cubed
- 2 tablespoons granulated sugar
- 1 cup all-purpose flour
- 2 large eggs
- 1 teaspoon vanilla extract
- Vegetable oil spray
- 1/4 cup granulated sugar
- 1 teaspoon ground cinnamon

Directions:

1. Prepare the dough: In a saucepan, combine water, butter, and 2 tablespoons sugar. Bring to a boil over medium heat. Remove from heat and immediately whisk in flour. Stir vigorously until a dough forms and pulls away from the sides of the pan. Let cool slightly, about 5 minutes.
2. Whisk in eggs: Once cooled slightly, beat in eggs one at a time, mixing well after each addition. Stir in vanilla extract.
3. Fill the piping bag: Transfer churro dough to a piping bag fitted with a star tip (about 1/2 inch opening).
4. Preheat air fryer: Preheat your air fryer to 375°F (190°C). Lightly spray the basket with vegetable oil spray.
5. Pipe the churros: Pipe 3-4 inch churros directly into the preheated air fryer basket, leaving space between them. Alternatively, pipe churros onto a parchment-lined baking sheet and freeze for 30 minutes before air frying.
6. Cook the churros: Air fry for 15-20 minutes, flipping halfway through, or until golden brown and crispy. Cooking time may vary depending on your air fryer model.
7. Make the cinnamon sugar: While the churros cook, combine 1/4 cup sugar and cinnamon in a bowl.
8. Coat and serve: Immediately after cooking, roll the hot churros in the cinnamon sugar mixture to coat. Serve warm with your favorite dipping sauce, such as chocolate sauce, caramel sauce, or whipped cream.

Nutritional Information per serving estimated: Calories: 200, Fat: 8g, Saturated Fat: 5g, Cholesterol: 30mg, Sodium: 130mg, Carbohydrates: 25g, Sugar: 15g, Protein: 3g

Tips:

- For extra crispy churros, preheat your air fryer for 5 minutes at 400°F (200°C) before lowering the temperature to 375°F (190°C) for cooking.
- Don't overcrowd the air fryer basket, as this can prevent even cooking. Cook in batches if necessary.
- If your churros aren't browning evenly, rotate the basket halfway through cooking.

Strawberry Shortcake Biscuits:

Prep Time: 10 minutes | **Cook Time**: 8 minutes | **Total Time**: 18 minutes | **Servings**: 4

Ingredients:

- 1 1/2 cups all-purpose flour
- 2 tablespoons granulated sugar
- 2 teaspoons baking powder
- 1/2 teaspoon baking soda
- 1/4 teaspoon salt
- 1/2 cup cold unsalted butter, cubed
- 1/2 cup buttermilk
- 1/4 cup milk
- 1 tablespoon melted butter (optional, for brushing)
- Fresh strawberries, hulled and sliced
- Whipped cream, for serving

Directions:

1. Preheat: Preheat your air fryer to 350°F (175°C). Lightly grease or spray your air fryer basket.
2. Dry Ingredients: In a large bowl, whisk together flour, sugar, baking powder, baking soda, and salt.
3. Cut in Butter: Using a pastry cutter or your fingers, cut the cold butter into the dry ingredients until the mixture resembles coarse crumbs.
4. Wet Ingredients: In a separate bowl, whisk together buttermilk and milk. Add the wet ingredients to the dry ingredients, stirring just until combined. Be careful not to overmix, as this can result in tough biscuits.
5. Shape and Air Fry: Gently shape the dough into 4 equal biscuits. Place the biscuits in the preheated air fryer basket, ensuring they don't touch. Brush the tops with melted butter, if desired.
6. Cook: Air fry for 8-10 minutes, or until golden brown and cooked through.
7. Assemble and Serve: Let the biscuits cool slightly. Split each biscuit in half horizontally. Arrange the bottom halves on serving plates. Top with fresh strawberries and whipped cream. Enjoy immediately!

Nutritional Information per serving: Calories: 250, Fat: 10g, Saturated Fat: 6g, Cholesterol: 30mg, Sodium: 250mg, Carbohydrates: 35g, Sugars: 15g, Protein: 4g

Tips:

- For extra fluffy biscuits, use self-rising flour and omit the baking powder and baking soda.
- Don't overwork the dough, as this can make the biscuits tough.
- If you don't have buttermilk, you can make your own by adding 1 tablespoon of lemon juice or vinegar to 1/2 cup milk and letting it sit for 5 minutes.
- For a fun twist, add a handful of chocolate chips or dried fruit to the dough before shaping.
- You can substitute other fruits for the strawberries, such as blueberries, peaches, or raspberries.

Pineapple Upside-Down Cake

Prep Time: 10 minutes | **Cook Time:** 20-25 minutes | **Total Time:** 30-35 minutes | **Servings:** 4-6

Ingredients:

- 1 can (8 oz) sliced pineapple rings, drained (reserve 1 tablespoon juice)
- 4 maraschino cherries, optional
- 1/2 cup packed light brown sugar
- 1/4 cup (1/2 stick) unsalted butter, melted
- 1 box (15.25 oz) yellow cake mix
- 1 egg
- 1/3 cup vegetable oil
- 1/4 cup milk

Directions:

Preheat: Preheat your air fryer to 320°F (160°C). Lightly grease a 6-inch round cake pan or ramekins.

1. Pineapple & Brown Sugar: Arrange pineapple rings in a single layer on the bottom of the prepared pan. Place a maraschino cherry in the center of each ring, if using. Sprinkle evenly with brown sugar.
2. Cake Batter: In a large bowl, whisk together cake mix, reserved pineapple juice, egg, oil, and milk until smooth. Pour the batter evenly over the pineapple and brown sugar in the pan.
3. Air Fry: Place the pan in the air fryer basket and cook for 20-25 minutes, or until a toothpick inserted into the center comes out clean.
4. Cool & Invert: Let the cake cool in the air fryer for 5 minutes. Carefully invert the cake onto a plate, allowing the warm pineapple and caramel sauce to drizzle down. Serve warm or at room temperature.

Nutritional Information per serving: Calories: 350, Fat: 14g, Saturated Fat: 7g, Cholesterol: 40mg, Sodium: 180mg, Carbohydrates: 42g, Sugar: 28g, Protein: 3g

Tips:

- For a richer flavor, use dark brown sugar instead of light brown sugar.
- You can substitute fresh pineapple slices for the canned ones. Use thicker slices for a more substantial texture.
- If you don't have maraschino cherries, you can use other toppings like chopped nuts or a drizzle of caramel sauce.
- To make individual servings, use ramekins instead of a cake pan. Bake for 10-12 minutes, or until a toothpick inserted into the center comes out clean.
- Leftovers can be stored in an airtight container in the refrigerator for up to 3 days.

S'mores Crescent Rolls:

Prep Time: 10 minutes | **Cook Time:** 8-10 minutes | **Total Time:** 18-20 minutes | **Servings:** 8

Ingredients:

- 1 can (8 ounces) refrigerated crescent rolls
- 1/4 cup chocolate chips
- 1/2 cup mini marshmallows
- 1/4 cup graham cracker crumbs (optional)
- 1 tablespoon melted butter (optional)
- Chocolate sauce, for drizzling (optional)

Directions:

1. Preheat your air fryer to 375°F (190°C). Lightly grease the basket with cooking spray or brush with melted butter.
2. Separate the crescent dough into 8 triangles.
3. Place a dollop of chocolate chips (about 1 teaspoon) on the wide end of each triangle.
4. Top with a few mini marshmallows (4-5 each).
5. Sprinkle with graham cracker crumbs (optional) for added texture and flavor.
6. Carefully roll up the crescent rolls starting from the wide end towards the point, enclosing the filling.
7. Brush the rolls lightly with melted butter (optional) for a golden brown finish.
8. Arrange the rolls in the air fryer basket, leaving space between them for even cooking.
9. Air fry for 8-10 minutes, or until golden brown and the marshmallows are melted and gooey.
10. Drizzle with chocolate sauce (optional) and serve warm.

Nutritional Information per serving: Calories: 200, Fat: 9g, Carbohydrates: 24g, Protein: 2g, Sugar: 15g

Tips:

- For a richer flavor, use Nutella or peanut butter instead of chocolate chips.
- Add a pinch of cinnamon or sea salt to the graham cracker crumbs for extra pizazz.
- If your marshmallows brown too quickly, cover the basket with foil for the last few minutes of cooking.
- Let the rolls cool slightly before serving to avoid burning your mouth.

Air Fryer Brownies

Prep Time: 10 minutes | **Cooking Time**: 15-20 minutes | **Total Time**: 25-30 minutes | **Servings**: 4-6

Nutritional Information per serving: Calories: 320, Fat: 18g, Saturated Fat: 10g, Carbohydrates: 32g, Sugar: 25g, Protein: 4g, Sodium: 120mg

Ingredients:

- 1/2 cup all-purpose flour
- 1/4 cup unsweetened cocoa powder
- 1/2 teaspoon baking powder
- 1/4 teaspoon salt
- 1/2 cup unsalted butter, melted
- 1 cup granulated sugar
- 2 large eggs
- 1 teaspoon vanilla extract
- 1/2 cup chocolate chips (optional)

Directions:

1. Preheat your air fryer to 325°F (163°C). Lightly grease a small oven-safe baking pan or ramekins with cooking spray.
2. Whisk together dry ingredients: In a medium bowl, whisk flour, cocoa powder, baking powder, and salt.
3. Combine wet ingredients: In a large bowl, whisk together melted butter, sugar, eggs, and vanilla extract until smooth.
4. Combine wet and dry ingredients: Gradually add the dry ingredients to the wet ingredients, mixing until just combined. Do not overmix.
5. Fold in chocolate chips (optional): Gently fold in chocolate chips, if using.
6. Pour batter: Pour batter into your prepared pan or ramekins, spreading evenly.
7. Bake: Place pan or ramekins in the preheated air fryer and bake for 15-20 minutes, or until a toothpick inserted into the center comes out with a few moist crumbs. (Cooking time may vary depending on your air fryer model and pan size.)
8. Cool and serve: Let brownies cool in the pan for a few minutes before transferring to a wire rack to cool completely. Serve warm or at room temperature with your favorite toppings, such as powdered sugar, chocolate sauce, ice cream, or whipped cream.

Tips:

- For a fudgier brownie, reduce the baking time by a few minutes.
- For a cakier brownie, bake for the full time or even a few minutes longer.
- You can use different types of chocolate chips, such as milk chocolate, dark chocolate, or white chocolate.
- For a richer flavor, use high-quality cocoa powder.
- Be sure not to overmix the batter, as this can lead to tough brownies.
- Let the brownies cool completely before cutting and serving, as they will firm up as they cool.

Cinnamon Sugar Pretzel Bites

Prep Time: 15 minutes | **Cooking Time:** 8-10 minutes | **Total Time**: 23-28 minutes | **Serving Size:** 12-15 bites

Ingredients:

Pretzel Dough:
- 1 cup warm water (105-110°F)
- 1 packet (2 ¼ teaspoons) active dry yeast
- 1 tablespoon granulated sugar
- 1 tablespoon canola oil
- 1 teaspoon salt
- 2 ½ cups all-purpose flour, plus extra for dusting
- Cinnamon Sugar Coating:
- 2 tablespoons unsalted butter, melted
- ¼ cup granulated sugar
- 2 teaspoons ground cinnamon

Directions:
1. Make the Pretzel Dough: In a large bowl, combine warm water, yeast, sugar, and oil. Let stand for 5 minutes, until foamy. Stir in salt and 2 ¼ cups flour until a shaggy dough forms. Turn out onto a lightly floured surface and knead for 5-7 minutes, adding more flour as needed, until smooth and elastic. Place dough in a greased bowl, cover with plastic wrap, and let rise in a warm place for 1 hour, or until doubled in size.
2. Shape the Pretzel Bites: Punch down dough and divide into 12-15 equal pieces. Roll each piece into a rope about 8-10 inches long. Cut each rope into 3-4 pieces, creating small pretzel pieces.
3. Prepare the Baking Soda Bath: Preheat your air fryer to 400°F. Bring a pot of water to a boil. Stir in 1 tablespoon baking soda. Working in batches, carefully drop the pretzel bites into the boiling water for 30 seconds each. Use a slotted spoon to remove and transfer to a wire rack to drain.
4. Air Fry the Pretzel Bites: Arrange the drained pretzel bites in a single layer in your air fryer basket. Do not overcrowd the basket, as this will prevent even cooking. Air fry for 8-10 minutes, or until golden brown and slightly puffed.
5. Coat with Cinnamon Sugar: While the pretzels are air frying, melt the butter in a small bowl. In another bowl, combine the sugar and cinnamon. Once the pretzels are cooked, brush them with melted butter and then roll them in the cinnamon sugar mixture to coat evenly.
6. Serve Warm: Enjoy your Cinnamon Sugar Pretzel Bites immediately while they are warm and soft. They can be served as is, or with your favorite dipping sauce, such as honey mustard or cream cheese dip.

Nutritional Information: Calories: 180, Fat: 7g, Carbs: 24g, Protein: 4g

Tips:

- For a chewier pretzel, use only bread flour instead of all-purpose flour.
- You can adjust the amount of cinnamon sugar to your liking.
- If you don't have an air fryer, you can bake the pretzel bites on a preheated baking sheet at 400°F for 10-12 minutes, or until golden brown.
- Store leftover pretzel bites in an airtight container at room temperature for up to 2 days. They can be reheated in the air fryer for a few minutes to refresh them.

CONCLUTION

It's time to look back on the delectable meals we've produced, the abilities we've developed, and the memories we've made in the kitchen as we near the finish of our culinary adventure through the Complete Air Fryer Recipes Cookbook. This cookbook has been a celebration of taste, inventiveness, and the fun of cooking with an air fryer, with everything from crispy appetizers and savory main dishes to decadent sweets and sweet delights.

We've explored the many possibilities of air frying, trying out new recipes, reimagining old favorites, and spending special meals with loved ones throughout this cookbook. We've been astounded by the air fryer's adaptability since it can turn basic ingredients into crispy, golden-brown treats using a fraction of the oil needed for more conventional frying techniques.

But this cookbook has been more than just a collection of recipes—it's been an investigation and learning experience. We now know that air frying has several advantages over deep frying, including being a healthier method of cooking and yielding incredibly crispy food without all the mess and trouble. We've welcomed exploration and innovation, attempting novel flavor pairings and customizing recipes to our preferences.

Along with honing our culinary talents, we've mastered methods for precisely preheating, seasoning, and cooking as we've explored the realm of air frying. We've embraced the art of recipe conversion, finding new ways to enjoy our favorite foods with a healthy twist by modifying classic recipes to fit the air fryer.

Above all, however, this cookbook has been a voyage of connection and community. The recipes in this cookbook have encouraged moments of pleasure, laughter, and shared experiences by bringing us together around the table, whether we are cooking for our family, friends, or ourselves. The act of preparing and sharing a meal has evolved into a beloved ritual in today's fast-paced society, serving as a gentle reminder of the value of slowing down, living in the present, and providing nourishment for both body and spirit.

I hope this cookbook inspires you to keep air-frying and to experiment with new tastes, recipes, and methods with a sense of wonder and excitement as you turn the last page. In the realm of air frying, there's always something new to learn, and the culinary options are unlimited, regardless of your level of experience.

So use this cookbook as a reference as you go out on new culinary endeavors, and may every meal you produce make you happy, fulfilled, and proud of yourself. I appreciate you coming along on this trip with me, and happy cooking!

FREQUENTLY QUESTION

Can I use parchment paper or aluminum foil in my air fryer?

- ✓ Yes, you can use parchment paper or aluminum foil in your air fryer, but it's important to use perforated parchment paper or foil with holes to allow for proper air circulation. This helps to prevent obstructing airflow and ensures even cooking. Make sure to trim the paper or foil to fit the air fryer basket and avoid covering the entire surface to allow the hot air to circulate effectively.

How much oil should I use in my air fryer?

- ✓ Air fryers require much less oil than traditional frying methods. Generally, you only need a small amount of oil to lightly coat your ingredients, usually about 1-2 teaspoons for most recipes. Using a spray bottle or brush to evenly distribute the oil can help achieve a crispy texture without excess oil. Some recipes may not require any oil at all, especially if the ingredients are naturally high in fat.

How do I clean my air fryer?

- ✓ Cleaning your air fryer regularly is important to maintain its performance and prevent buildup of grease and food residue. Most air fryers have removable parts, such as the basket and tray, that can be washed with warm, soapy water or placed in the dishwasher if they are dishwasher-safe. Wipe down the interior and exterior of the air fryer with a damp cloth or sponge to remove any food particles or grease. Be sure to consult the manufacturer's instructions for specific cleaning guidelines.

Can I cook frozen foods in my air fryer?

- ✓ Yes, you can cook frozen foods in your air fryer. Frozen foods such as french fries, chicken nuggets, and fish fillets can be cooked directly from frozen in the air fryer. Adjust the cooking time and temperature according to the instructions provided on the packaging or based on your air fryer's settings. Cooking frozen foods in the air fryer is convenient and can result in crispy, delicious results without the need for preheating or thawing.

Can I bake in my air fryer?

- ✓ Yes, you can bake a variety of foods in your air fryer, including cakes, muffins, cookies, and even bread. Air fryers function as miniature convection ovens, circulating hot air around the food to cook it evenly. When baking in the air fryer, use oven-safe baking pans or molds that fit inside the air fryer basket. Adjust the temperature and cooking time as needed based on the specific recipe and the size of your air fryer.

Can I use cooking spray in my air fryer?
- ✓ Yes, you can use cooking spray in your air fryer, but be mindful of using it sparingly to avoid excess residue buildup. It's best to spray the food lightly before cooking to help achieve a crispy texture.

Can I reheat leftovers in my air fryer?
- ✓ Yes, you can use your air fryer to reheat leftovers. Simply place the leftover food in the air fryer basket and heat it at a low temperature (around 320°F or 160°C) for a few minutes until warmed through.

How do I prevent food from sticking to the air fryer basket?
- ✓ To prevent food from sticking to the air fryer basket, lightly coat the basket with oil or cooking spray before adding the food. You can also use parchment paper or aluminum foil with holes to line the basket and prevent sticking.

Can I cook raw meat in my air fryer?
- ✓ Yes, you can cook raw meat in your air fryer. Ensure that the meat is properly seasoned and trimmed of excess fat before cooking. Follow recommended cooking times and temperatures to ensure that the meat is cooked safely and thoroughly.

How do I know when my food is done cooking in the air fryer?
- ✓ You can check the doneness of your food by using a food thermometer to measure the internal temperature. Additionally, visually inspect the food to ensure that it is golden brown and crispy on the outside.

Can I use foil packets in my air fryer?
- ✓ Yes, you can use foil packets in your air fryer to cook vegetables, fish, or other delicate foods. Make sure to leave some space around the foil packet to allow for proper air circulation.

How do I season my air fryer basket?
- ✓ To season your air fryer basket, lightly coat it with oil and heat it at a low temperature (around 300°F or 150°C) for about 5-10 minutes. This helps to create a non-stick surface and prevent food from sticking during cooking.

Can I bake bread in my air fryer?
- ✓ Yes, you can bake bread in your air fryer. Use oven-safe bread pans or molds that fit inside the air fryer basket, and adjust the temperature and cooking time as needed based on the specific recipe.

Can I cook bacon in my air fryer?

- ✓ Yes, you can cook bacon in your air fryer. Arrange the bacon slices in a single layer in the air fryer basket and cook at 400°F (200°C) for 8-10 minutes, flipping halfway through, until crispy.

How do I clean the heating element of my air fryer?

- ✓ To clean the heating element of your air fryer, allow it to cool completely, then use a damp cloth or sponge to wipe away any food residue or grease. Avoid using abrasive cleaners or scrubbing tools that could damage the heating element.

Can I cook frozen vegetables in my air fryer?

- ✓ Yes, you can cook frozen vegetables in your air fryer. Simply place the frozen vegetables in the air fryer basket and cook at a high temperature (around 400°F or 200°C) for 10-15 minutes, shaking the basket halfway through, until tender and crispy.

How do I prevent my air fryer from smoking?

- ✓ To prevent your air fryer from smoking, make sure to remove excess oil or fat from the food before cooking. Avoid using too much oil or cooking at too high of a temperature, as this can cause smoking. Additionally, regularly clean the air fryer basket and tray to prevent buildup of grease.

Can I use metal utensils in my air fryer?

- ✓ It's best to avoid using metal utensils in your air fryer, as they can scratch the non-stick coating of the basket or tray. Instead, use wooden, silicone, or plastic utensils to avoid damaging the surface.

Can I cook multiple types of food at the same time in my air fryer?

- ✓ Yes, you can cook multiple types of food at the same time in your air fryer by using a divider or placing different foods in separate compartments of the basket. Just be mindful of cooking times and temperatures to ensure that each type of food cooks properly.

How do I prevent the air fryer from overheating?

- ✓ To prevent the air fryer from overheating, make sure that there is adequate ventilation around the appliance and avoid blocking the air vents. Additionally, avoid overloading the basket with food, as this can restrict airflow and cause overheating.

Can I make popcorn in my air fryer?

- Yes, you can make popcorn in your air fryer using popcorn kernels and a little bit of oil. Simply place the kernels in the air fryer basket, drizzle with oil, and cook at a high temperature (around 400°F or 200°C) for 8-10 minutes, shaking the basket occasionally, until the popcorn pops.

How do I store my air fryer when not in use?

- When not in use, store your air fryer in a cool, dry place away from heat sources and direct sunlight. Make sure to unplug the appliance and allow it to cool completely before storing it. Store any removable parts, such as the basket and tray, separately to prevent damage.

Can I use my air fryer to dehydrate foods?

- Some air fryer models come with a dehydrating function that allows you to dehydrate foods like fruits, vegetables, and herbs. Follow the manufacturer's instructions for using the dehydrating function and adjust the temperature and cooking time as needed based on the specific food.

Can I use my air fryer to roast coffee beans?

- While it's technically possible to roast coffee beans in an air fryer, it's not recommended due to the risk of uneven roasting and potential damage to the appliance. It's best to use a dedicated coffee roaster or oven for roasting coffee beans.

Can I use my air fryer to proof bread dough?

- Yes, you can use your air fryer to proof bread dough by setting it to a low temperature (around 90-100°F or 30-38°C) and placing the covered dough inside for the desired proofing time. This helps to create a warm, humid environment that encourages yeast activation and dough rising.

GLOSSARY

Air Fryer:
- A kitchen appliance that cooks food by circulating hot air around it at high speed, producing a crispy exterior similar to frying but with less oil.

Convection:
- The process of heat transfer in which hot air circulates around the food, cooking it evenly and efficiently.

Crispy:
- A texture achieved when food is cooked to a golden-brown, crunchy exterior while remaining tender inside, often associated with fried foods.

Preheat:
- To heat the air fryer to the desired cooking temperature before adding food, ensuring even cooking and optimal results.

Temperature Control:
- The feature in an air fryer that allows the user to set and adjust the cooking temperature according to the requirements of the recipe.

Cooking Time:
- The duration for which food is exposed to heat in the air fryer, determined based on the recipe and desired level of doneness.

Basket:
- The removable compartment of the air fryer where food is placed for cooking, typically made of non-stick material and perforated to allow air circulation.

Non-Stick Coating:
- A layer applied to the surface of the air fryer basket and tray to prevent food from sticking during cooking and make cleanup easier.

Parchment Paper:
- A paper with a non-stick surface that can be used to line the air fryer basket, preventing food from sticking and making cleanup easier.

Aluminum Foil:
- A thin, flexible metal sheet that can be used to cover food in the air fryer, help retain moisture, and facilitate even cooking.

Crumbs Tray:
- The removable tray at the bottom of the air fryer that collects crumbs, drippings, and excess oil during cooking, making cleanup easier.

Heating Element:
- The component of the air fryer that generates heat and circulates hot air around the food, facilitating cooking.

Oven Mitts:
- Protective gloves worn when handling hot air fryer components, such as the basket and tray, to prevent burns and injuries.

Overcrowding:
- Placing too much food in the air fryer basket, which can obstruct airflow and result in uneven cooking and less crispy results.

Seasoning:
- Adding herbs, spices, or other flavorings to food before cooking to enhance its taste and aroma.

Doneness:
- The state of being fully cooked or prepared to the desired level, typically determined by visual inspection or using a food thermometer.

Reheating:
- The process of warming up leftover food in the air fryer to make it hot and ready to eat.

Ventilation:
- The circulation of air within the air fryer, essential for proper cooking and preventing overheating.

Food Thermometer:
- A kitchen tool used to measure the internal temperature of food to ensure it is cooked safely and thoroughly.

Baking:
- The process of cooking food in the air fryer using dry heat, typically at a lower temperature than frying, to achieve a tender texture.

Deep Frying:
- A cooking method that involves submerging food in hot oil to cook it quickly and create a crispy exterior.

Dehydrating:
- The process of removing moisture from food using low heat and airflow, often used to preserve fruits, vegetables, and herbs.

Roasting:
- A cooking method that involves cooking food in the air fryer at a high temperature to achieve a caramelized exterior and tender interior.

Searing:
- Browning the surface of food quickly at a high temperature to seal in juices and enhance flavor.

Proofing:
- Allowing bread dough to rise before baking, often done in the air fryer at a low temperature to create a warm, humid environment.

Preheating:
- Heating the air fryer to the desired cooking temperature before adding food, ensuring even cooking and optimal results.

Glaze:
A sweet, often glossy coating applied to food, such as pastries or meats, to add flavor and moisture.

Dredging:
- Coating food in flour, breadcrumbs, or other dry ingredients before cooking to add texture and flavor.

Marinating:
- Soaking food in a seasoned liquid, such as a marinade or sauce, to enhance its flavor and tenderize it before cooking.

Printed in Great Britain
by Amazon